P9-ARY-038

Columbia University

Contributions to Education

Teachers College Series

No. 259

AMS PRESS
NEW YORK

THE MEASUREMENT OF
EARLY LEVELS OF INTELLIGENCE

BY

KENNETH S. CUNNINGHAM, Ph. D.

TEACHERS COLLEGE, COLUMBIA UNIVERSITY
CONTRIBUTIONS TO EDUCATION, NO. 259

BUREAU OF PUBLICATIONS
Teachers College, Columbia University
NEW YORK CITY
1927

Library of Congress Cataloging in Publication Data

Cunningham, Kenneth Stewart, 1890–
 The measurement of early levels of intelligence.

 Reprint of the 1927 ed., issued in series: Teachers
College, Columbia University. Contributions to edu-
cation, no. 259.
 Originally presented as the author's thesis, Columbia.
 Includes bibliographical references.
 1. Mental tests. 2. Child study. I. Title.
II. Series: Columbia University. Teachers College.
Contributions to education, no. 259.
BF431.C8 1972   155.4'23   72-176701
ISBN 0-404-55259-5

Reprinted by Special Arrangement with Teachers
College Press, New York, New York

From the edition of 1927, New York
First AMS edition published in 1972
Manufactured in the United States

AMS PRESS, INC.
NEW YORK, N. Y.   10003

ACKNOWLEDGMENTS

The writer desires to express his feeling of indebtedness to those whose direct or indirect assistance has contributed to the work here reported.

His introduction to and interest in psychology date back to the work done under and with Mr. J. McRae, M.A., at that time lecturer in psychology at the Melbourne Teachers' College, and Professor W. R. Boyce Gibson, of Melbourne University.

As members of the Teachers College advisory committee for the present investigation, Professor L. S. Hollingworth, Professor H. T. Woolley, and Professor H. A. Ruger have given readily of their time in discussing procedure and offering helpful suggestions. In particular Professor Ruger contributed invaluable guidance in the statistical treatment as well as in the discussion of the significance of the results. In the early stages the work was planned along lines discussed fully with Professor R. Pintner, whose absence on leave during later stages deprived the writer of a continuance of his stimulating help.

A special debt is owed to Professor E. L. Thorndike, who not only made the investigation possible by making the test material available but very freely gave personal help at points where it was needed—help which was all the more appreciated because of the writer's tendency to take up theoretical positions which Professor Thorndike might not himself agree with.

Without the indirect assistance and encouragement of his wife the work could not have been carried out. She also contributed a considerable amount of direct help in matters of correction and tabulation.

K. S. C.

CONTENTS

THE MEASUREMENT OF
EARLY LEVELS OF INTELLIGENCE

CHAPTER I

THE INVESTIGATION AND ITS SIGNIFICANCE

The provision in recent years of fairly satisfactory and easily used, and misused, scales for the measurement of intelligence supplied such a badly felt want that the total amount of attention given to making and applying them has been far greater than that given to a careful examination of the presuppositions upon which they are based. In a very apt simile Spearman has recently spoken of tests as miners excavating forward into wonderfully rich new ground but repeatedly missing the correct direction on account of laboring in darkness.

The whole mental testing movement has of course been dominated by the greatness of the pioneering work done by Binet. His method was to take measurements of abilities varying in range from those which are largely perceptual and factual to those which are highly conceptual and symbolic. By a process of summation of what is achieved out of groups of tests which are all given equal weight we arrive at a general estimate of the individual's ability which we express in a score called his mental age.

As contrasted with Binet's method we have that of taking a particular kind of ability, such as that to give opposites, and arranging a scale increasing in difficulty so that we can ascertain the part of the scale beyond which a given individual cannot go. This method is obviously more informative and accurate, so far at least as the ability or abilities tested are concerned. In the Binet Test, for example, if a child cannot successfully name four colors our scoring assumes that in that task he is still at least twelve months removed from the ability to do so and, further, that he deserves an equal, namely a zero, score whether he has correctly named one, two, or three of the colors. This weakness of tests built on the 'all or none' pattern has been frequently pointed out. Burt[1] referring to the mode of construction of the

[1] Burt: *Mental and Scholastic Tests*, p. 4.

Binet Test says, "It is unfortunate that the serial gradation of the same test was not adopted systematically for every specific function and carried without a break through every mental age."

The interesting question arises as to whether if we adopt the carefully graded method we can do with fewer samplings from the total range of abilities in getting a reliable estimate of the individual's general intellectual maturity. In general, group tests assume that this is possible, but there is a considerable divergence of practice in the selection of the types of abilities to be measured.

For diagnostic purposes the thing which we most wish to know about an individual is where he stands in comparison with those with whom he can most justly be compared. Hence we rank him with reference to the hypothetical 'average' individual of his own age. Since mental tests originally were intended, and still are used, primarily for diagnostic purposes, the scaling of tests on the age-scale plan has been the one usually adopted. As we shall see later, one inherent limitation of this method is that it tells us nothing of the real amount of development which equal increases in test score represent. This applies particularly to mental age scores and somewhat similarly to scores on group tests.

To provide a continuous scale which will be free from some of the limitations of most of our tests, a large amount of work has been done at the Institute of Educational Research at Teachers College, Columbia University, under the direction of Professor E. L. Thorndike. The result is a test which aims at providing a complete scale for the measurement of ability in completions, arithmetic, vocabulary, and directions (in brief the CAVD Test) which will be extensive enough to cover all ranges in the abilities in question from those which are only just measurable to those which approach the upper limits of human capacity. Those responsible for the test have spoken of it as measuring "CAVD intelligence" as a recognition of the fact that it depends on ability in one out of a number of possible combinations of types of test. They do not doubt the advisability and the eventual probability of adding parallel tests of other functions. At the same time there can be no doubt that its lack of width is offset by its searching character as a test of general ability.

Rather than attempt to grade every single task in strict order of difficulty throughout, the devisers of the CAVD Scale have grouped them into 'levels' each consisting of ten tasks of approximately equal difficulty. Thus there is Level A in arithmetic and each of the other three tests, making a total of 40 tasks at this, the easiest level. Similarly there are 40 tasks at Level B and at Level C and at each of the higher levels. Levels A to E inclusive require individual and oral testing; the higher levels can be used as group tests.

Thus it will be seen that an individual who does all the tasks in Levels A to E attempts a total of 200 items of which 50 are completions, 50 are arithmetic, 50 are vocabulary, and 50 are directions tests. A detailed idea of the nature of the tasks at these levels may be obtained from an inspection of the samples given in Appendix I. We will give here a brief general account of the tests.

Completions Test. The completions test requires the subject to supply the missing word in a spoken sentence. Practice examples assist the subject in getting the 'idea' of what he is to do.

Arithmetic Test. The arithmetic test involves simple quantitative knowledge and manipulation. Ability to count, to show a named number of objects, to name a shown number of objects, to compare sizes of objects presented or referred to, to give the result of adding or subtracting small numbers when the components are shown concretely but the result of the operation is hidden, and, in Level E, simple problems, are the types of abilities tested.

Vocabulary Test. The vocabulary test is in picture form. The pictures are presented in groups of five and for each such group the child is asked to point to the object which is named. Occasionally the same set of five is repeated and the subject asked to indicate a different object, but for most of the words a different set is used.

Directions Test. The directions test consists of a number of simple instructions which the subject is asked to carry out. With the exception of all but a few in Level A, the response is a pencil and paper one and thus leaves a permanent record. In using the pencil at Level A the subject is asked to do little but imitate a ring, a line, and a cross which are made in front of him. In Level B he is asked to do these things without a model but is shown how to do them after a failure. In higher levels no such assistance is given and the subject is asked to carry out simple markings of this kind in more complicated situations. In some cases success or failure depends on the ability to profit by the opportunities for learning which the first two levels give.

It is not proposed, even if the writer were capable of doing it, to discuss in detail the mode of construction, the theoretical implications, and the importance for intelligence testing of these CAVD tests. These matters are fully dealt with in a book which has recently been published.[2]

The present investigation concerns itself solely with the earliest levels of the test, viz., A, B, C, D, and E. It is also limited to work with young children and derives its chief significance from the fact that the tests at these levels were worked out with adults as subjects. In all cases the original subjects were more than twelve years of age chronologically and this means that most of them were at imbecile levels of intelligence. The CAVD Scale was primarily intended for the measurement of all ranges of adult ability; it was not assumed that it would necessarily be a valuable instrument for use with young children. So many interesting questions are involved, however, that it seemed that it would be very well worth while to see what would happen if the test were applied to normal children at mental levels equivalent to those of the adults.

Some of the questions on which some light may be obtained are as follows: Can we obtain a satisfactory measurement of developing intelligence at early levels by the use of inferior adult mentality as a criterion? Does the relative difficulty of the simplest tasks for an intelligence which has reached its fullest development remain the same for an intelligence which has reached a corresponding development at a much earlier age? In other words, does a given 'mental age' mean the same thing, even so far as nothing but intellectual difficulty is concerned, in the case of individuals whose chronological ages vary widely? If certain tasks stand out as markedly easier or more difficult for the children than for the adults, will these tasks appear to have certain characteristics in common? If the instrument appears successful for the measurement of ability (at least of the abilities which the test involves) in young children, what will be suggested as to the relative size of the increments made in passing through the dif-

[2] Thorndike: *The Measurement of Intelligence.*

ferent stages of development? In other words, if the test provides a scale in which the steps are steps of equal difficulty, can we from its results make inferences as to the nature of the curve which represents the growth of intelligence? Apart from general questions of this kind it will be interesting to see if any light is thrown on the early development of the functions which the test employs. From the point of view of test administration, workers in the field will be interested in the provision of another scale for the early levels of intelligence and will wish to know whether this new scale is reliable, capable of easy application, and so on.

Where such fundamental questions as the true nature of the concept of mental age, the true rate of growth of intelligence, the existence or non-existence of qualitative differences in mental processes are concerned, it would be folly to expect that an investigation as slight as the present one would do more than throw a faint glimmer of light here and there.

Our present test scales seek to measure individuals by a method which could be compared to the attempt to ascertain physical size by seeing which of a number of ready-made suits of clothes provide the best fit in general. The scales of the future will undoubtedly be more comparable to the method of ascertaining total physical size by accurate measurements of certain bodily dimensions taken on graded scales. Which particular 'dimensions' are to be chosen and how they should be combined into a total score will provide the psychologist with much to discuss long after the scales themselves are constructed.

COLLECTION OF DATA

The results to be reported in this study are based on the testing of 257 cases by means of Levels A to E of the CAVD Scale. Of these, 5 were not completed for one reason or another and another 5 cases were older than the highest age group used in the general statistical treatment. It was the original intention to have age groups of 50, each group covering a range of six months, the total range extending from $2\frac{1}{2}$ to $5\frac{1}{2}$ years. It proved impracticable, however, to complete this number in the two lowest age groups, partly because a large number of children below and some children above three years of age cannot satisfactorily be tested with a test of this kind involving a great deal of verbal work. As indicated previously all the testing with these levels is individual in character; the average length of time taken to test one case would work out at close to one hour for the CAVD tests.

In the case of 103 of the children the Stanford Binet Test was given in addition, either at the same time as, or within a few days of, the CAVD tests. All of the foregoing tests, with the exception of about a dozen of the CAVD tests, which were given by a thoroughly competent examiner, were applied by the writer. In 16 additional cases Binet or Kuhlmann results were available from previous tests and, assuming constancy of I.Q., the mental ages at the time of giving the CAVD tests were calculated, thus giving 119 cases in which it was possible to compare Binet mental age and CAVD score.

The plan was to get a fair enough sampling of children at each age to try out the range of the test's applicability as well as to obtain very tentative norms for the various ages. For some purposes, however, we are more interested in the results of normal and superior children.

Since it could not safely be assumed that, for example, a task in Level E on the adult results would not come down to Level B for children, the whole of the tasks in Levels A to E were given to each child. This was done in almost all cases except where such a procedure was obviously unnecessary; for example, when a child failed in a test upon which a later test directly depended.

No uniform procedure was adopted as to the subdivision of the entire examination into sittings. At times it was found possible to give both Binet and CAVD at one sitting without any apparent loss of interest and attention on the part of the child. At times three sittings were required to complete the CAVD alone. The conditions for testing were as a rule quite suitable. As in all such work with young children, there were cases where the coöperation of the child was not fully obtained or where it was indifferently maintained. The number of cases where serious factors of error are introduced through this cause is probably small. In order to make a study of the various types of test attitudes, notes were taken on all cases and a scheme for recording these was worked out and is given and discussed in Appendix II.

SOURCES OF DATA

The subjects were drawn from three main sources. Table I indicates how they were distributed among these sources, and Binet I.Q.'s and CAVD scores give some suggestions as to the general nature and relative standing of the samplings.

TABLE I

ANALYSIS OF THE POPULATION TESTED

Age Groups Years	PUBLIC SCHOOLS			DAY NURSERIES			PRIVATE SCHOOLS		
	No. of Cases	Mean I.Q.	Mean CAVD	No. of Cases	Mean I.Q.	Mean CAVD	No. of Cases	Mean I.Q.	Mean CAVD
2½–3				3		16	9	132 (3)	51
3–3½				24	99 (7)	32	7	124 (5)	77
3½–4				28	94 (13)	50	18	120 (8)	93
4–4½	4		83	31	97 (21)	68	12	131 (8)	130
4½–5	13	96 (3)	85	28	104 (21)	96	9	125 (9)	125
5–5½	32		126	20	94 (8)	113	5	118 (5)	134
Totals & Means	49	96 (3)	98	134	94 (70)	63	60	125 (38)	102

Note: The figure in brackets given under each mean I.Q. represents the number of cases upon which the mean was calculated. The mean CAVD scores were based upon the total numbers in the groups, since every child had this test.

Table I shows that 49 of the children tested attended public schools in New York City, 134 of the cases were in Day Nurseries in various parts of the city, and the remaining 60 cases were attending private schools. The great majority of the last group were children in attendance at the Horace Mann and the Speyer Nursery Schools.

The Day Nursery Schools are semi-charitable institutions

where the children of working mothers are cared for throughout the day. These schools do not admit cases of obvious mental deficiency, but since on the whole the children in them come from homes of inferior economic standing, we would not expect the general intellectual ability of the children to be quite normal, so far at least as we can judge it accurately from our mental tests. It will be seen that the results bear out this expectation. The two lowest age groups are obviously not fair samples of the total population of these ages; they represent children below average ability. The age groups above these probably can be regarded as more typical samplings and as giving more reliable results as we pass to higher ages.

Owing to the large amount of language work in the test, it was felt to be desirable to avoid cases where there was a handicap in this direction and children whose parents spoke a language other than English were not tested when this fact was known.

CHAPTER II

GENERAL RESULTS OBTAINED

We shall first take up the question of the general impressions and results which were obtained through the application of the test and shall occupy ourselves later with a more minute analysis of the difference between the performances of the children and those of the original adult subjects. We shall thus at first tend to be occupied with questions as to the practical applicability and suitability of the test for young children as well as the possibilities which a test of this kind opens up. The later treatment will tend to lead us to a somewhat more theoretical discussion as to possible differences of quality in mental processes.

ATTRACTIVENESS OF THE TEST

The CAVD Test suffers somewhat in general attractiveness for young children when compared with the Binet Test with its frequent changes and introduction of new material. It would seem that this is an almost necessary result of any test which seeks to get an exhaustive measurement of particular functions. The repetition of tasks of the same kind and in some cases of the identical tasks in the CAVD Test was felt at times to detract from maximum effort and in a few cases led to a quite unemotional but nevertheless quite determined refusal to attempt a particular task a second or a third time. This difficulty was, as a rule, limited to the arithmetic tasks, where some of the series are repeated three times in order to avoid chance successes and to give the subject an opportunity of profiting from the practice which the series provides. In the case of a number of children the repetition had this effect but in other cases it was felt that the child's first effort was quite definitely the best indication of his true ability. In some cases it was possible to complete the series by returning to them later; but in other cases, where a definite and fixed antipathy was sensed, the child was marked on the basis of a single repetition of the series.

On the whole, however, the scale suffers far less from this weakness of unattractiveness than one would expect. The whole of the vocabulary test being in picture form very rarely presents any difficulty; the directions test very seldom fails to attract and hold the child interested owing to its opportunity for the use of pencil and paper. The completions test at times loses interest for the child but not as a rule until he has reached levels where he is out of his depth. Negativistic attitudes are not infrequently brought about by the Binet Test or parts of it, and it may be doubted whether such factors of uncertainty, even if more frequent in the case of the CAVD Test, are not more than counterbalanced by its more searching character.

CORRELATIONS BETWEEN CAVD AND BINET

It will be interesting to inquire as to the amount of correspondence between these two tests in the 119 cases where both tests were applied. The correlations obtained by the Pearson product-moment formula between CAVD scores and Binet mental age and between each of the component parts of the CAVD Test taken separately and Binet mental age are given in Table II.

TABLE II

CORRELATIONS—CAVD SCORES AND BINET MENTAL AGE

	r	P.E.
Binet M.A. and Total CAVD	.925	.009
Binet M.A. and Completions	.815	.021
Binet M.A. and Arithmetic	.849	.017
Binet M.A. and Vocabulary	.793	.023
Binet M.A. and Directions	.824	.017

The correlations reported in this table are of course remarkably high; they are in fact as high as the self-correlations of some of the widely used tests. It is particularly interesting that, as in the case of the arithmetic test, the correlation between a more or less specialized form of ability and a test of a very general kind, such as the Binet, should rise as high as .85.

In a general way the Binet and the CAVD have more in common than might appear at first sight. Both involve a preponderance of language work, both depend largely on oral replies, both introduce a certain amount of arithmetical knowledge, both make some use of pictures and depend a great deal on general information. But the range of abilities included in the Binet is much the wider of the two. There is nothing in the CAVD to correspond with the memory tests, the comprehension tests, the discrimination of colors, and so on.

As in all other cases the correlation must be interpreted in the light of the total range of ability of the cases tested and the variability within the arrays of the correlation table. The total men tal age range would extend from about 2½ to 7½ years. Figure I gives a graphical representation of the variability in mental age which was found to be associated with given ranges of CAVD score. For example, those obtaining CAVD scores of more than 39 but less than 50 obtained mental age scores ranging all the way from 36 to 46 months. It is thus easy to see that if we know a child's CAVD score and wish to predict from it what his mental age is likely to be, we shall have to be satisfied with a prediction within certain limits of probability. The standard error of estimate gives us for the table as a whole a statement of the degree of probability within which we can predict values of one variable from given values of the other variable. Calculating[1] the standard error of estimate made in predicting M.A. from CAVD score, we find that it is 4.6 months. This means that taking a range of once the standard error on each side of the regression line we can say that the chances are two out of three that our prediction will be correct within 4½ months of mental age.

When the means of the arrays were plotted, they seemed to fulfill the requirement of rectilinearity of regression upon which the ordinary correlation formula depends; but since there was a suggestion of curvilinearity at the two extremes of the distribution the correlation ratios were worked out. The two ratios are as follows: $\eta_{xy} = .93$ and $\eta_{yx} = .89$. Summing up on the question of the comparison between Binet and CAVD tests, we can say that the CAVD may safely be used as an alternative for the Binet, provided, as always, that the results are interpreted in the light of the limits of probability indicated by the standard error of estimate.

[1]From the formula: $\sigma_M = \sigma_C \sqrt{1 - r^2_{M.C}}$ where M stands for M.A. and C for CAVD Score.

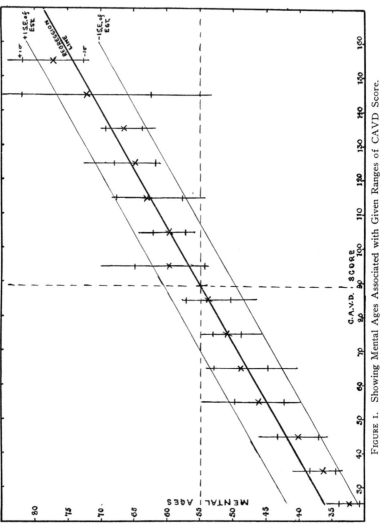

FIGURE I. Showing Mental Ages Associated with Given Ranges of CAVD Score.
The line for the regression of mental age on CAVD score is shown and, on each side
of this, a distance corresponding to the standard error of estimate.

CAVD SCORES OF SUCCESSIVE AGE GROUPS

We must next turn to the internal evidence which the test has to offer as to its general suitability. Table III gives a general picture of the results obtained by each of the six-months age groups. The second column gives the mean chronological age of each group. It is not to be expected that the means of these groups would lie exactly at the mid-point of the interval in each case. Only in the case of the highest group, however, does it lie more than a fraction of a month away. Some indication of the average Binet mental age of each group can be obtained from the fourth column, which gives the mean mental age of the cases in each group on which Binet test results were available, the number of such cases for the group being indicated in brackets.

The next two columns give the mean CAVD score for each group in two forms. In the first form it is simply based on the total score obtained by each child when we add together his successes at each level. In the next column the results are given in

TABLE III

MEAN CAVD SCORES BY C.A. GROUPS

Age Group	No. of Cases	Mean C.A.	Mean M.A.	Mean Total	Scores Altitude	Mean Scores on Levels				
						A	B	C	D	E
2½–3	12	2.9	3.4 (4)	42	24.21	24.4	12.4	4.6	.6	0
3 –3½	31	3.2½	3.6 (14)	42.6	24.26	22.3	12.4	5.1	1.8	.5
3½–4	46	3.8½	3.10 (22)	66.6	25.90	29.1	19.8	10.7	3.6	2.6
4 –4½	50	4.2¾	4.6¾ (32)	85.2	26.98	33.1	24.4	15.5	7.9	4.4
4½–5	51	4.8¾	5.2 (34)	96.9	27.29	34.8	28.1	18.1	10.0	5.8
5 –5½	57	5.3¾	5.4¾ (13)	122.2	29.02	38.1	33.6	23.5	16.9	10.7

the form of altitude scores based on the table of altitudes provided in the test blank. This table of altitudes aims at giving us a means of knowing the equivalent values for a given score in any one of the levels. It gives the altitude values of scores from 5 to 35 on any level from A to H. Thus a score of 5 is given a value of 20.0 in A, of 23.2 in B, of 25.3 in C, of 26.7 in D, and so on. Similarly a child who gets a score of 6 would be given an altitude score of 20.2 if he got it in Level A, 23.4 if he got it in Level B, 25.5 if in C, 26.9 if in D, and so on. Altitude values are not given for scores below 5 or above 35 because it is considered that, in the first case, chance successes and, in the second case, chance failures would tend to receive too much weight.[2] Let us suppose, then, that a child has scores as follows out of the possible 40 at each level, 25 in A, 18 in B, 10 in C, 5 in D, and 3 in E. In order to give his total performance a single numerical value in the table of altitudes we could convert each raw score into its corresponding altitude score and then get an average of these. This would, however, be rather laborious in practice and it is suggested in the test instructions that the calculation be based on those two levels in which the subject's total most nearly approaches 40. In the sample case given the two adjacent levels to be used are A and B since the combined score on these two levels is 43, whereas on B and C it would only be 28. Taking then his score of 25 in A we see that it has an altitude value of 23.8 and his score of 18 in B an altitude value of 25.9. Averaging these we get 24.8 as an expression of the total merit of his performance. This method really means that we limit our consideration of the subjects ranking to his performance on the 80 items comprised in those two levels which for him lie at the most critical part of the scale. In very rare cases the method seems to do something in the nature of an injustice. Suppose a subject has made a score of 35 in B, 20 in C, and 10 in D. According to the given method of scoring, his altitude score is to be based on his scores in C and D; it is, however, slightly higher if based on B and C, and this would be done if the subject had scored 6 less on Level D. It thus means that the subject could

---

[2] The construction of a table such as this is based on the conversion of raw scores into scores in terms of the standard deviation of a given population, a method which has been elaborated by McCall in *How to Measure in Education*. The present test employs a modification of this method which is explained in the book by Thorndike mentioned above.

have got a higher altitude score by doing fewer of the tests correctly.

On the whole the ranking based on the method given above correlates so highly with the simple total raw score on the whole test that for most purposes it appears to be legitimate to use either indifferently. Since the total score is easier to handle arithmetically, we have used it in most parts of this study.

If the age groups were free from errors of sampling, we could take the mean scores as giving norms on the test for the ages in question. A glance at the column giving the mental ages suggests, however, that the CAVD scores are higher than they would be for unselected age groups. This impression must in turn be modified by the fact that Binet tests were given rather more frequently, in proportion to the number of cases, in the private school group than in the other groups. There is, as we would expect, a steady rise in the mean score made by each successive age group.

A more searching mode of examination will be to ascertain what each age group does on each of the levels. The necessary facts are given in the last five columns of Table III and are graphically represented in Figure 2. We would have expected a drop in the average score obtained as we passed to each higher level, but it will be seen from the graph that the decrease is one of remarkable steadiness. The flattening at the two ends is what is to be expected from the fact that the simplest tasks are too easy to differentiate between the children in the oldest age group and that the most difficult tasks are too difficult for the youngest children. In other words, the youngest age groups are really measured only by Levels A, B, and C, while the oldest age group is measured most satisfactorily on Levels C, D, and E. We can say, then, that over the levels where the tests are suitable for the children the average decrease in raw score made on successively higher levels is an almost constant quantity. A fact related to this can be brought out by an examination of the number of individual cases where the subject has actually scored higher on a more 'difficult' level than he did on a lower one. Table IV gives this information and shows the actual scores of all cases who made a higher score on a higher level than they did on a lower one.

From Table IV it may be seen that out of all the cases tested

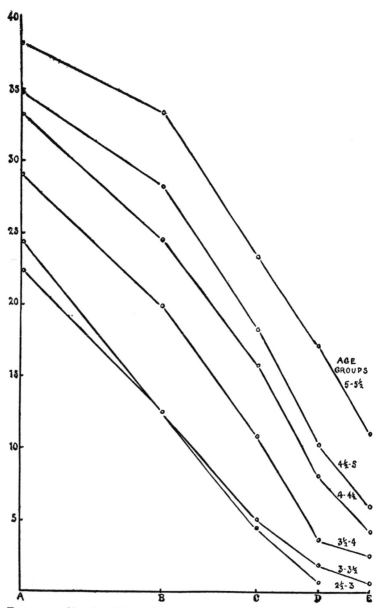

FIGURE 2. Showing Mean Scores on CAVD Levels Obtained by Each
Chronological Age Group.

The levels are placed at distances corresponding to those represented in the table
of altitudes.

TABLE IV

Scores of Those Scoring Higher on Higher Levels

Age Group	Scores on Levels				
	A	B	C	D	E
2½–3	No	cases			
3 –3½	No	cases			
3½–4	37	31	14	5	6
4 –4½	38	36	29	14	16
4½–5	34	22	15	10	11
	39	38	23	8	18
	33	18	5	0	3
	39	35	29	17	20
5 –5½	39	37	30	31	26
	39	36	27	9	15
	39	38	34	23	28

only nine failed to lose in score in passing from each level to the next higher one. In eight of these cases the level which gains over the one before it is Level E. Most of the gains are but slight. In the one case where there is a really big gain, viz., one of 10, analysis of how the gain was obtained shows that it was built up about equally of gains in the arithmetic, the vocabulary, and the completions tasks. It is quite possible that if the original data on the imbeciles were available and were analyzed in the same way we would find as many examples of individuals who reversed the usual procedure and scored slightly higher as they passed to higher levels. On the whole the evidence suggests that the increments of difficulty represented in the grouping of the tasks into levels on the basis of adult performance constitute very similar increments of difficulty for children of the same ranges of mentality.

As a final mode of presenting the general results we can ascertain what happens when we convert into altitude scores the actual scores obtained by each age group on the various levels. This would be most accurately done by taking each individual in the group separately, converting his scores on each level into altitude scores, and then averaging for the group. Since, however, we are interested only in the general trend of the results it will be sufficiently accurate for our purpose to adopt the much quicker method of taking the average raw scores which are graphically represented in Figure 2 and simply converting these into their equivalents on the table of altitudes. The results of doing this are given in Figure 3. The chief point of interest here is the question as to the consistency of the altitude score obtained by any one group on the different levels. If the relative difficulty

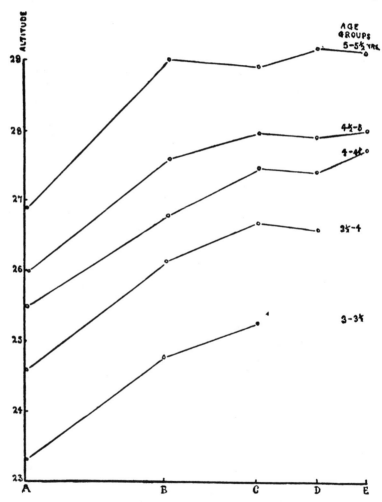

FIGURE 3. Showing, on Successive Levels, the Altitude Equivalents of Mean Total Scores Obtained by Each C.A. Group.

of the levels for the groups of children remains the same as it was for the adults, we will on the whole expect a fairly constant altitude score for a given group. Examination of the graph shows that this is realized more for the older than for the younger groups and more for the other levels than for Level A and, to a less degree, Level B. The general inference suggested is that relative to the other levels Level A is considerably easier for the children than for the adults.[3] We shall, however, leave until a later stage a fuller discussion of this and other differences between child and adult performances.

[3] At first sight it would appear that the drop in altitude score on Levels A and B for the children indicates that these levels are relatively more difficult for the children than for the adults, but reflection shows the reverse to be the case. If the table of altitudes were constructed on the basis of the children's performances, we would, in order to preserve a constant altitude level for a given group, have to move up the altitude equivalents in A and B for a given score. This would mean that we would bring Level A far closer to Level B, and Level B a great deal closer to Level C for children than it is for adults. This means that for children these levels are less difficult in relation to the others than the situation represented in the given table of altitudes implies.

CHAPTER III

EXAMINATION OF THE SEPARATE TESTS IN THE SCALE

It will be worth while to consider the question of the separate development of the abilities which are employed in the CAVD Test. It may well be that the various functions the sum total of which is often thought of as making up intelligence have different rates of development; or, if we adopt the view that intelligence should be identified with some central factor which is more or less involved in various functions, one might regard it as probable that the special factors are, amongst other things, differentiated by the different rates at which they approach maturity. Whatever then may be our conception of the nature of intelligence, it seems open to conceive of different rates and periods of development within those varied abilities which form the complicated pattern of our mental life. The curves by which maturity is reached in height, weight, physiological maturity, and so on are not at all identical: we can, and often do, put on more weight after height is at its maximum. It is quite conceivable that, in the same way, a curve showing the development of our ability to master arithmetical combinations and number facts may behave in a different way from a curve showing the growth of our vocabulary. The discovery of facts of this kind would be of much psychological interest and might have great pedagogical importance.

We have examined our data from this point of view in order to see whether any suggestions can be obtained. We can do this by adding each child's results for each test instead of each level, thus getting his score on all the tasks in directions, in vocabulary, in arithmetic, and in completions, each separately. We find, for example, that a child's total score of 68 is made up of 18 obtained on directions, 20 on vocabulary, 14 on arithmetic and 16 on completions. Another child's total score might be constituted quite differently; in fact, even in the youngest age groups, the differences are often great enough to suggest genuine specialization of ability rather than a merely accidental unevenness of score. We can, however, find what the average performance of a given age group is on each test and the rate at which the average score increases as we pass to each higher age group.

The results of this mode of examining the data are given in Figure 4. We shall discuss this and at the same time make certain observations about each of the tests in the scale.

DIRECTIONS TEST

With the exception of the youngest age group it will be observed that the highest scores are made on the directions test throughout. The alterations in relative position of the scores of the two youngest groups are interesting since these groups have about equal mental ages, the younger group being more highly selected. The actual drop in vocabulary and completions suggests that at a young age precocity shows itself most distinctly in language development, since it is probably in these two tests that success is most directly dependent on ability to understand and use language. The big increase in directions score in passing from the youngest group to the next one does not appear likely to be the result of a purely intellectual difference. It may well be the result of the inability of children below three years of age to fall in with the (to them) rather artificial situation of waiting for, listening to, and carrying out verbal instructions when they have before them the fascinating possibilities of pencil and paper. That the score on directions should consistently be higher than on the other tests is an interesting matter. We shall see later on that it is in this test that the scores of the children are furthest removed from those of the adults.

ARITHMETIC TEST

The scores on the arithmetic test are distinctly the lowest for the first three age groups, but the rapid rise in scores which takes place from then on causes the scores eventually to pass all the others except those in directions. Normal and bright children of mental ages up to about four have sometimes scarcely commenced to count, to be able to show a named number of objects (2, 3 or 4 being asked for), or to name a shown number of objects. It must of course be recognized that a child may be intellectually capable of making number distinctions and combinations before he has acquired the number names by which we

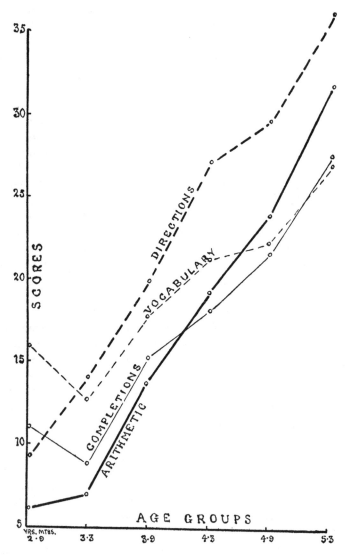

FIGURE 4. Showing Increments Obtained by Successive Age Groups on Each Test Taken Separately.

adults label the various groupings. Some of our bright children apparently failed to achieve success in certain unseen additions and subtractions merely because they could not give the correct name to the result, as, for example, when they indicated the answer by holding up the correct number of fingers. It is obvious from observation that a very young child can tell the difference between two objects and one object of the same kind, and probably three objects and two objects, before he has begun to speak at all. It is interesting to observe from our results, then, that it does appear possible for correct mental manipulation to take place with such comparatively unlabeled number groupings, —though we would not expect it to run very far ahead of ability to name the groups. It would be interesting if one could devise tests of number appreciation as distinct from number naming and trace the extent of the parallelism between the two abilities in young children of different degrees of intelligence. Apparently the progress of most normal children is marked from about three years on by a rapid development in the grasp of conventional and fundamental number facts.

VOCABULARY TEST

It will be noticed that the curve for the picture vocabulary test scores changes from highest of the curves at the youngest age to lowest of the curves at the highest age. Its range of development is least in comparison with the other abilities tested. In considering this matter we must, however, bear in mind the fact that the test is not an ordinary vocabulary test and we must hesitate to draw inferences from its results as to the development of the vocabularies of children. In the first place, being in picture form, it is limited to the testing of the names of objects and thus does not sample at all attributive and relational words.

One's first tendency is to think that a test of vocabulary in picture form would necessarily be easier than a test of the same words in ordinary oral form. It is undoubtedly easier to administer, but a moment's reflection will show that it is not necessarily easier in itself. It all depends on the form which the picture vocabulary test takes. If a child is asked to point to the picture of a named object which is included in a series along with four other pictures, his success or failure will be determined in the first place by his knowledge of the word itself, but even if he 'knows' the word he may still fail because of the fineness of the discrimination which he is asked to make in choosing the correct picture. Thus with this form of test (apart from the question of the suitability of the picture itself) the difficulty depends not only on the words for which the subject is being tested but also on the words which are chosen as decoys.

If the subject does not know the word, there is one chance in five that any particular picture, including the correct one, will be chosen. (This is not strictly true since in any set of five pictures one is likely to be more attractive or striking than the others, and if this one should happen to be the correct one the results obtained are misleading. There is some suspicion that this happened with one of the words in our series.) There is also the chance that an intelligent subject, not knowing the word asked for but knowing the names of all the objects but one, may choose this one by a process of intelligent elimination. From their 'thinking aloud' we are convinced that a few of our bright subjects obtained an occasional success this way.

It seemed that it would be worth while to attempt to find out whether the factors making for ease in obtaining successes on the test, viz., chance, intelligent elimination, and general ease of response, made this type of test easier or more difficult than would have been an ordinary oral test of the same words. To obtain some light on this question a check-up was carried out on the vocabulary test results of a number of children. In these cases, after the test had been given in the ordinary way, the child was questioned in the style of the Stanford-Binet vocabulary test on all the words on which he had failed as well as on the words on which there was any suspicion that he had succeeded without knowing the word. We can then count up the number of cases in which there were successes without knowledge of the word and compare this with the number of cases in which there were failures in spite of knowledge of the word. In 43 cases in the oldest age group where the oral testing was carried out we find that the total number of 'chance' successes was 133, while the number of failures when the child 'knew' the word was 237. Owing to various factors of error we are not justified in regarding these figures as being more than very approximately correct, but the difference is so marked that there can be no doubt that as a test of word knowledge the test in its present form is more difficult than it would be in oral form. The inference is not by any means that the test would be better in oral form, but merely that we must be cautious in making assumptions as to knowledge of particular words from a vocabulary test in this form.

COMPLETIONS TEST

It was felt that the chief interest to be derived from the completions test result lies in a demonstration of the fact that it is apparently possible to apply this type of test to young children in an oral form. Only a very few cases with mental ages probably below three failed to get the idea of supplying the missing word in an incomplete sentence. Completions tests have proved themselves so useful in the measurement of intelligence that it should be of interest to trace the early development of the abilities involved. It should be noted that many forms of test, both verbal and non-verbal, may be cast into completions form; it seems better, however, to limit the name to those which adhere as closely as possible to the type originally devised by Ebbinghaus. The essence of such tests seems to be that the subject must appreciate (it is a matter of vague 'feeling' rather than conscious apprehension) the relationship between the given parts in such a way that an appropriate completion is brought to mind. As in most types of tests there appear to be two desiderata in this type of test. In the first place we should avoid dependence on any knowledge which might favor one individual as against another. In no intelligence tests can we completely achieve this ideal, but the various forms of some of our most valuable tests derive whatever is specific about them from the fact that the informational requirements are made as constant and as non-critical as may be for all subjects.

In the second place we should seek to get examples where the part to be supplied is as determinate as possible, partly because one has the feeling that these would be the best measures of intelligence, and partly so that we will not be faced with the difficulty of adjudicating upon shades of merit in the answers between which it is almost impossible to discriminate.

An inspection of the A to E completions tasks and of the children's answers shows that these difficulties arise to some extent, but it may well be that they become progressively more difficult to avoid as we get down to lower levels of intelligence. It would be interesting to see whether it would be possible to construct a very simple completions test in narrative form, as used by Ebbinghaus. It would probably be more attractive to children than separate sentences and while still using very simple material we could increase the difficulty and the determinateness of the omissions by virtue solely of accumulated relationships with previous parts of the narrative. So far as our present test is concerned the informational elements involved are of a very general nature. Except possibly in one or two instances (e.g., "We go to church on . . . ."), they do not appear calculated to favor one individual rather than another or adults rather than children.

In some of the examples it was not at all easy to adjudicate on the answers received. In this connection it is interesting to notice that on the whole the children showed far greater fertility of response than did the imbeciles. All the doubtful answers were rated independently by the writer and a psychologist of much experience in the construction and marking of tests. Out of a total of 145 that were in any way doubtful there was agreement between the judges in all but 36. These were decided on by discussion and the assistance of a third examiner. This element of doubt in the marking of the completions test would not in any appreciable way affect the total score of individuals since the average number of doubtful answers per individual would not be over four. It would be even less for answers where adjudication was truly arbitrary, and to some extent doubtful passes would balance doubtful failures.

An examination of the curve for completions shows a fairly steady development for the age groups. This suggests that there is no general unsuitability of the test for children, although, of course, it is possible that other examples might be found which would discriminate between them even better than the present ones do. It is interesting to note that there is a general tendency toward a change in the grammatical function of the omitted part as we pass from lower to higher levels. We shall examine later on the particular examples in which the performance of the children differed significantly from that of the adults.

CHAPTER IV

THE GROWTH OF INTELLIGENCE

One of the things which psychology would most like to know is the precise nature of the curve which, particularly during the early stages of life, most accurately represents the growth of intelligence. The solution of this matter is, however, beset with many difficulties. Our physical measurements of growth and maturity do not typically show quite regular curves; over certain periods of life growth is characteristically accelerated or retarded. It is unsafe to argue from analogy, but we must at least keep our minds open to the possibility that something similar takes place in mental development.

We are able to ascertain irregularities in rate of physical growth because we set up arbitrary but constant standards of, let us say, length, and can thus ascertain increments for given periods of time in terms of the constant standards we have decided on. In mental development the case is far more complicated. In the first place, we are satisfied for all but the most extremely philosophical purposes that we know what we mean by 'length', but we are far from any general agreement as to what we mean by 'intelligence', especially when it comes to a question of choosing or constructing an instrument which measures it unambiguously. Further, we feel no hesitation about using feet and inches for measuring either infants or adults without discrimination, but we find that no single test (we are not referring to a single type of test) of intelligence is of value over more than a few years of mental development. If we wish to measure a man taller than our longest measuring stick, we can do so by simply adding more units of the kind we had been using; and we could, if we wished, invert our measure to obtain the height of an infant by the same units of the scale which we added to get the height of the tallest individual. Obviously we cannot transpose the parts of our mental measurements in this way, so that eventually we are not at all sure how far we have got from the ground when we arrive at tests which, for example, discriminate between one college graduate and another.

27

Various writers have recognized that tests built on the age-scale plan cannot from their very mode of construction give us information on this matter of the relative size of the increments in ability made on the average in each successive year of life. For example, Gesell[1] puts the position thus: "If we attempt to state the increments of development in terms of absolute time units we shall come to the untenable conclusion that one year of development at any age is equal to one year of development at any other age."

Similarly Kuhlman[2] is of opinion that "the amount of mental development during a year cannot be taken as an accurate unit of measurement of intelligence."

We do not wish to enter into a full discussion of the numerous investigations and speculations which have attempted to throw light on this question. We shall be satisfied with opening up a few of the main issues. Numerous references to relevant works will be found in the study of this question by Teagarden, whose own research related particularly to the upper end of the developmental curve.[3] An important summary of researches and discussion of possibilities will be found in a recent book by Freeman, who concludes "that there are certain narrow and specialized capacities which have their own rate or period of development and that these culminate at somewhat different stages. During the period at which these abilities are developing, however, they appear to develop at a fairly constant rate."[4] He thus disagrees with the rather widely held view that the curve representing the growth of intelligence should be a logarithmic one.

Perhaps the chief advocate of this view has been Woodrow, who thinks that we have evidence that "a mental age at the younger ages means a bigger change than it does at the higher ages."[5] In support of this he cites Bobertag's finding that the increase in percentage of children passing a certain test is twice as great between the ages of 7 and 8 as between the ages of 11 and 12. On facts of this kind he thinks we are justified in

---

[1] Gesell: *The Mental Growth of the Pre-School Child*, p. 17.

[2] Kuhlman: Results of Examining Public School Children. *Journal of Psycho-Asthenics*, Vol. 18, 1914, p. 235.

[3] Florence M. Teagarden: *A Study of the Upper Limits of the Development of Intelligence.* Teachers College, Columbia University, Contributions to Education, No. 156.

[4] Freeman: *Mental Tests*, p. 342.

[5] Woodrow: *Brightness and Dullness in Children*, p. 46.

assuming that the growth of intelligence should be represented by a curve which rises most rapidly during the early years of life and, gradually losing acceleration, reaches its maximum at some age not yet agreed upon. In fact, in an article[6] he claims that by weighting tests in proportion as they differentiate between successive age groups, i.e., by weighting most heavily those tests which give the smallest amount of overlapping in the percentage of successes obtained, and summing the results, we are able to obtain a curve "showing the absolute increase in intelligence of children with increase in chronological age." It would seem necessary that several points be established before it could be agreed that this method automatically does what it is claimed to do. We are obviously weighting the tests in proportion as they indicate growth of some kind, but it does not appear that it is necessarily growth in intelligence which receives the greatest weight. Further, as Freeman points out in the book referred to, decreasing rate of mental growth is not the only possible cause of increase in overlapping of scores as we pass to higher ages; straight but divergent lines of yearly development will give the same result. He sums up: "The age growth curve seems to approach much more nearly a straight line than a logarithmic curve within the limits of those ages for which a particular test is well suited and up to the period of adolescence."[7]

Before we consider any possible relation of our own work to this problem there is one other difficulty which must be discussed a little more specifically. We have referred to the fact that we cannot take the units from one part of our scales for mental measurement and use them indifferently in any other part, as we can with our feet and inches. This is due to two reasons. In the first place we do not measure intelligence directly as a quantity; what we do is to estimate its amount by seeing what it enables an individual to 'do', and as we progress up the scale of mental life we have gradually to alter the things which we ask individuals to do or else we would not get any differences in performance at all as we got much above or below our original starting point. In the second place we do not measure intelligence in abstraction from everything else; we unavoidably approach it through the medium of experience and seek to render this con-

[6] Arthur and Woodrow: An Absolute Intelligence Scale. *Journal of Applied Psychology*, Vol. 3, 1919, p. 118.
[7] *Op. cit.*, p. 281.

stant by employing only those elements which everyone's experience has given them a chance to acquire.

Some writers have been considerably exercised about this matter, since, as, from definition, experience is something which alters with age, it is possible to hold that the variation in this factor makes it impossible to justly take tests standardized on one age group and use them to discriminate between members of another age group. The matter is discussed at length by Chapman and Dale,[8] who point out that in individual examinations we give to precocious children of nine years of age the tests which have been devised and justified only for children of, let us say, twelve years of age, whereas the test procedure used by Terman only establishes the fact that the test element is valid for children of approximately that chronological age in the neighborhood of its particular age position. "It would appear," they say, "that the use of the mental age method of measurement while practically straightforward is subject to such inherent defects that for finer work in the realm of intelligence measurement it must eventually be displaced. A child of eight and a child of twelve cannot be compared. It is impossible to select test elements which are not affected by the additional four years of environmental influence enjoyed by the latter child. Eventually we must state the performance of the x-year-old in terms of the performance of a large group of x-year-old children, using either percentiles or distances in terms of sigma."

We have discussed these matters on account of their more or less direct bearing on the question of the possibility of the use of the CAVD Scale for finding out facts regarding the growth of intelligence. It is obvious that this and similar scales which should give us much information about the total distribution of adult intelligence will be the means of giving us more information about the nature of the curve of intelligence in its upper reaches; whether we can legitimately use it for the early levels of intelligence is not quite so easy a matter to decide. We at least avoid the difficulty inherent in using successive age groups of children; we appear, however, to run rather deeply into whatever difficulties are involved in the attempt to use the tests for a different chronological age group from that on which the tests were standardized.

[8] Chapman and Dale: A Further Criterion for the Selection of Mental Test Elements. *Journal of Educational Psychology*, Vol. 13, No. 5, pp. 267-276.

It is, then, a question as to whether we can use the low end of the total distribution of adult ability as a means of gauging the rate of growth of ability in children. The distance which the individual can pass along this scale, in terms of comparison with his fellows, or with himself at a different period, becomes a measure of his ability or of his progress. Many would feel reluctant to admit that we can measure the brightness of children in terms of the dullness of adults, and, later on, we shall have to discuss the problems involved in this in some detail. For the time being, however, let us see what the result will be of assuming that the comparison is legitimate. It may be argued that if we give a constant meaning to intelligence, wherever it is found, there is no theoretical objection to a comparison of the ability of young children with that of inferior adults, and to ascertaining the rapidity with which children at different ages pass through the stages representing all degrees of adult intelligence. If this is granted, the problem becomes chiefly one of obtaining tests which are an equally good measurement of intelligence for both groups,—if, indeed, this be anything more than a pious hope. Leaving until later a detailed discussion of the differences in the performance of the two groups, it is perhaps legitimate to argue that since the CAVD Test as applied to children correlates highly with a generally accepted criterion of intelligence, the Binet Test, we may accept it as depending to almost the same extent as does the Binet Test itself on intelligence, and regard the CAVD scores made by successive mental age groups as giving some indication of the relative size of the increments in intelligence made by the groups in question.

For whatever value it may have, then, we have plotted in Figure 5 the line which represents the increments in CAVD score made by the children when grouped according to mental age. The choice of the size of our class interval for mental age is arbitrary but is guided by two considerations. If we make it very small, we will have so few cases in each mental age group that the average CAVD score for the groups will not be very reliable. On the other hand, if we make it too large, it will mean that we are smoothing our curve and thus possibly concealing differences in rate of development which are significant. We have chosen four-month groupings in the attempt to avoid either of these extremes. In order to obtain some suggestion as to the reliability of the

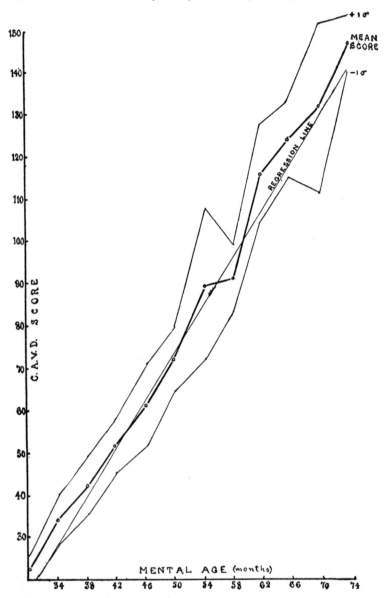

FIGURE 5. Showing Increase in Mean CAVD Score Obtained by Four-Month Mental Age Groups.

There is indicated the line showing regression of CAVD on mental age and also the standard deviations of the arrays of which the means are given.

mean CAVD scores for each group, we have plotted for each mean points representing plus and minus once the standard deviation of the CAVD scores obtained by the group. The lines joining these give a sort of band of probability within which the true line of regression may be expected to lie. It must of course be remembered that owing to the small number of cases—the whole table is based on only 119—the standard deviations of some of the age groups are themselves quite unreliable.

Another factor of uncertainty arises from the fact that the various levels in the CAVD Scale are not at equal distances of difficulty from one another, but, as represented in Figure 2, are at increasing distances as we pass from higher back to lower levels. In theory all the children were given the whole test; but in practice the younger children are measured only by the earlier levels, while the scores of the older groups depend largely on what they did on the upper levels. Since it is for adults, and possibly for children, more difficult to obtain a given score as we pass to each lower level, this may have the effect of decreasing to a slight but uncertain extent the apparent rate of development in the earlier mental ages from the slope we would get if the levels were at equal distances of difficulty from each other at all parts of the scale.

It will be observed that the general trend of the line we have obtained is practically straight. One would hesitate to say that there is any real significance in the minor irregularities, particularly in the marked slowing down between the mental ages of 4.6 and 4.10 and the less marked depression between 5.2 and 5.10. The period between 4.10 and 5.2, which is marked by the most rapid development, might be taken to have some connection with the entry into school of a large number of the cases in this mental age group; but it seems a little gratuitous to assume this when we have just before the acceleration a marked depression which obviously cannot be explained in the same manner.

SUMMARY

Summing up on this question we may say that it appears necessary to suspend final judgment until we can get repeated measures on the same individuals over a period of time. The question of the interpretation of curves of growth obtained by reference to a scale of adult intelligence will still remain. We could compare them with the curves obtained by reference to other standards of measurement. It might be held that even if such a scale is so unavoidably weighted for experience that we cannot take its results as an absolute measure of intelligence, we might still obtain from it a fairly accurate measurement of the relative sizes of the increments in intellectual development made during successive periods of life. It may even be that we need not worry unduly about the effect of experience where low levels of ability are concerned or that we will be able to get tests which are not as heavily weighted for experience as are some of our present scales.

CHAPTER V

COMPARISON OF NORMAL WITH INFERIOR INTELLIGENCE

GENERAL DISCUSSION

The primary interest in undertaking this investigation lay in the attempt to ascertain in detail what, if any, would be the differences between the performance on the test of young and old groups when we have children with mental ages equivalent to those of the adults. Before analyzing our results from this point of view it will be as well to discuss the various views which are held and the investigations which have sought to throw light on related problems.

The basic question is: Are there fundamental and characteristic differences between the intellectual processes of normal or superior intellects on the one hand and inferior intellects on the other? Or, to put the question in another form: Among the differences in mental processes which we find among individuals, are there any which increase in proportion as we move along the range of human ability and which seem to require for their explanation not merely the existence in greater or less amount of some one form of mental process but the existence of more than one type of intellectual functioning? We have put the question in this form so as to suggest the close relationship between two problems which have each been much discussed but which, so far as the writer is aware, have never been considered together. The first problem is: What is the nature of the differences between individuals of widely differing ability, i.e., between individuals of the same mental age but different chronological ages? The second problem is: Can we make a fundamental distinction (within any given individual) between types of mental process, in particular between 'association' and 'higher mental processes'? If there are genuine distinctions of higher and lower in the realm of mental, or, more narrowly, cognitive, activity, it is at least reasonable to suppose that individuals of good ability are distinguished from those of poor ability by the possession of greater facility in mental operations involving the higher processes.

These two problems have been held apart partly because of the different interests and angles of approach of those who have investigated them and partly because of practical difficulties in investigating them together. Those who have studied the differences between individuals of varying ability have usually done so without making *a priori* distinctions between higher and lower mental processes; though, as we shall see, they at times interpret their results in these terms. Those whose interest has been the rather more theoretical one of seeing whether the supposed distinction between association and higher mental processes can be maintained have, in the few cases where it has been a matter of investigation rather than theorization, chosen two groups of tests which appear to depend respectively on the two types of intellectual process and have sought to ascertain whether the performance of a given group of individuals on one set of tests will show a closer association with some criterion of intelligence than will their performance on the other set of tests. Thus in the one case we tend to rely more on the selection of our individuals, and in the other, on the selection of our tests. The matter tends to become largely a question of the degree of homogeneity within the group tested. If our groups have widely differing I.Q.'s with comparable M.A.'s, we will expect the clearest demonstration of any typical differences in mental process; but since our groups will differ greatly in chronological age, we have to meet the question of the actual effect, and the significance of the effect, of greater experience in the case of the older group. If our groups are more similar in C.A., we cannot include so wide a range of I.Q. because this would mean that the M.A.'s would become so different that the same tests could not be used.

DIFFERENCES BETWEEN NORMAL AND SUBNORMAL MINDS

What are the differences between subnormal and normal minds with reference to the types of intellectual process which they are best capable of carrying out? Is the difference merely one of amount or is it related to different forms of mental process which cannot fundamentally be reduced to variations in amount of some one still more basic process? In other words, are the bright distinguished from the dull not only, or perhaps not fundamentally, by how much they can do in any given intellectual task but by the fact that in certain forms of intellectual work of a higher type they stand markedly above their less fortunate fellows? Are the differences not merely quantitative, are they qualitative as well?

If we include both popular and scientific thought we have opinions on this matter ranging from one extreme to the other. Traditionally and historically the idiot and the imbecile have been regarded, and often treated, as being in a class which was apart, as being either sub- or super-human, according to the fashion of the time. It was thought that there was little or nothing in common between the normal and the abnormal mind.

Modern science has corrected this by stressing the continuity of mental life not only throughout the human race but throughout the whole gamut of living creatures. Many are prepared to accept the idea of a continuous distribution of intelligence from its lowest to its highest grades. In particular the concept of mental age has lent itself to the process of clearing away the popular and semi-mythical conception of a gulf lying between normality and subnormality, and has given us a sort of formula which is often accepted as a means of equating differences in chronological age.

It is fairly obvious that we need to introduce a number of qualifications into the concept of mental age or at least define carefully what we mean by it. A group of imbeciles of four-year-old 'mentality' will differ characteristically from a group of normal four-year-old children in a number of respects, with regard to behavior, motives, habits, social adjustments and so on. We must either not include these things in our concept of mental age or else not regard a given mental age as meaning the same thing, no matter where it is found. We are, however, concerned with only one aspect of mental life, viz., the more strictly intellectual in so far as it is measurable by actual or conceivable tests of intelligence. It may be that even with this limitation the term 'mental age' may act as a cloak which hides real differences.

On this as on some other matters quotations can be given from the writings of Binet which, if they do not actually contradict, at least seriously modify one another. For example, he claims that "il (l'anormal) n'est pas inferieur en degre, il est autre."[1] Again, in another book we find this statement: "This comparing of a backward intelligence to that of a child of a certain age might have passed ten years ago as simple literary comparison; but

[1] Binet et Simon: *Les Enfants Anormaux.*

since to-day we have acquired the power to fix within a few months at least the age of the intelligence of defectives, since we can with good reason consider a certain idiot of thirty years as the equivalent of a child of one, or an imbecile of twenty as the equivalent of a child of six, and since these defectives are so many children arrested in a certain phase of their development, we have only to arrange these defectives in an ascending series of evolution in order to make with it and because of it the psychogenesis of a function." [2]   But further on we read: "But it must be understood that this resemblance is only roughly true.   An imbecile of forty does not exactly resemble a normal child of five years; following the happy comparison of Kraepelin, he resembles him somewhat as would a caricature, he resembles him as much as an invalid can resemble a healthy person. . . . For the moment we shall not insist upon all the differences which obviously are numerous and which are, moreover, imperfectly known." [3]

Koffka[4] objects strongly to Binet's idea that one could replace the experiments upon children by experiments upon feeble-minded adults who might be considered as stereotyped children of a mesurable age.

Terman appears to stress the similarities rather than the differences between those of equal mental age and unequal chronological ages.   He writes:[5] "Previous to the publication of Binet's 1908 scale the significance of age differences in intelligence was very little understood.   Psychologists were not aware of the extraordinary and detailed similarity that may exist between a dull child of twelve years and a normal average child of eight." These quotations will serve to illustrate the wide differences of opinion which exist on this question.

We must now examine some of the chief investigations which bear more or less directly on the point at issue.   The Ordahls,[6] after carrying out tests in the attempt to ascertain differences between levels of intelligence, conclude: "In all experiments attention is involved and it is probable that this is the psychological process in which the levels of intelligence differ."

Chapman and Dale in the article previously referred to took a

[2] Binet: *The Intelligence of the Feebleminded*, p. 10.   (Trans. Elizabeth S. Kite.)

[3] p. 161.

[4] Koffka: *Growth of the Mind*, p. 33 footnote.

[5] Terman: *Genetic Studies of Genius*, p. 2.

[6] Ordahl and Ordahl: Qualitative Differences Between Levels of Intelligence in Feeble-minded Children, *Journal of Psycho-Asthenics*, Mono. Supp. Vol. 1, No. 2, 1915.

number of records on the National Intelligence Test and paired young bright children (under ten years) and old dull children (thirteen years and over) who got the same total score. They thus got two groups of the same mental age but different chronological ages. They assume that the ratio of performance of the young bright to the old dull group on a particular test gives an indication as to whether the given type of test depends more on native intelligence or on training. On this basis they arrange the sub-tests of the National Intelligence Test in order of their merit as tests of intelligence, giving them in the following order: opposites, sentence completion, logical selection, arithmetic problems, and symbol-digit substitution. They conclude that "the mentality of the young bright is different from that found in the old dull. It also shows that intellectual development is not marked by a simultaneous and uniform improvement in all types of mental function."

Merrill[7] analyzes the Binet test results of children of equivalent mental ages when grouped for differences of chronological age and makes inferences as to the mental processes involved in the tests in which the groups are characteristically successful. For example, her group with a mean mental age of six is broken into a retarded group with a mean C.A. of 9, a control group with a mean C.A. of 6, and a superior group with a mean C.A. of 4. The tests which contribute most to the scores of the retarded group are 'giving the number of fingers' and 'drawing a diamond,' while the failures of the same group are chiefly on 'differences' in year seven and on 'similarities' in year eight. She concludes that "those tests which are most difficult for the retarded are the ones which chiefly involve those functions which have ordinarily shown the highest correlations with intelligence. On the other hand the tests which contribute most to their score are those which depend more on information which may be acquired in the course of experience and a test involving as one element at least the manipulation of complex motor coordinations which is in part a function of life age." In summing up she concludes that "the relative difficulty of tests for normal retarded or superior differs characteristically. Tests involving the higher mental processes are the ones which contribute least to the mental age score of retarded children."

[7] Maud A. Merrill: *Comparative Psychology Monographs*, Vol. 2, September 1924.

Jones[8] reports a careful study designed to find out whether certain sub-tests in some of the most widely used test batteries depend on growth in C.A. rather than M.A. He uses partial correlation so as to render first C.A. and then M.A. constant. The sub-tests which, in their correlation with M.A. as measured by the median of the four tests used, are, with C.A. constant, nearest to 1.00 and, with M.A. constant, to o are taken to be those which give us the best measure of M.A. For combining these two criteria the coefficient of alienation method is used. The writer shows that the sub-tests do differ considerably when judged by these criteria. Some of the sub-tests which ranked high were information, sentence completion, analogies, and logical selection; while those which ranked lowest were visual comparison, symbol digit, fundamentals of arithmetic, and picture completion. It is further claimed that the results show that a particular test may be better adapted to the task of measuring intelligence at one level than at another.

We may in this connection finally refer to the conclusion reached by Burt [9] after ascertaining the correlation between a wide range of tests and intelligence as judged by teachers' ratings that "of the entire series of experiments ranging as it does from the lowest levels of mental processes to the highest the tests of the power of thinking, that is the power to understand or reason, are the best."

HIGHER AND LOWER MENTAL PROCESSES

It will readily be seen that much of the foregoing relates very directly to the question of making distinctions between higher and lower forms of mental process. There would probably be few who would object to regarding mental operations which are largely sensory or perceptual in character as lower than other more symbolic or abstract or 'intellectual' operations; but we get decided differences of opinion when it comes to the question of making similar distinctions within the intellectual realm itself. The debates on this matter have centered very largely round the question of the nature, the types, and the function of association in mental life. Everyone will remember James's treatment of

[8] Jones: *Effect of Age and Experience on Tests of Intelligence.* Teachers College, Columbia University, Contributions to Education, No. 203.
[9] Burt: Experimental Tests of Higher Mental Processes. *Journal of Experimental Pedagogy,* 1911, Vol. 1, pp. 93-112.

association by similarity as being based on association by contiguity.

A recent and important contribution to the discussion of the nature of the distinctions which may be made in the realm of cognition is that contained in a book by Spearman.[10] Here we have a very definite stand taken for a differentiation between what he calls the 'noegenetic' and the 'anoegenetic' mental processes, or, in other words, between those which relate to quality and those which relate to quantity. The elaboration of his noegenetic principles is really an attempt to state the laws which in his opinion govern the operation of the higher mental processes. It is probably fair to his position to seek to illustrate the distinction which he makes between the two types of mental process by reference to two types of mental test. In the first case let us suppose that the subject is read a list of familiar words, one at a time, and he is asked to respond with the first word that 'comes into his mind'; in the second case let us suppose that he has been given the same list of words but had previously been asked to give the opposite of each word as he heard it. The responses in the two cases would almost certainly be different, and it becomes a question of ascertaining the principles underlying the mental operations which cause the difference. Spearman would probably say that in the first case the responses are caused largely by quantitative considerations, such as the number of times the response word had previously occurred in association with the stimulus word; but that in the second case a new type of determination enters in, a type peculiar to the mental world, which is marked by the inevitability (unless the process goes astray) and, in some cases at least, the newness, for the individual, of the resulting item or its connection with the given one. Although in actual mental processes both quantitative and qualitative principles are held to operate, it is claimed that they are theoretically distinct and that they can in more or less pure form be illustrated by examples from the realm of mental testing. Further than this it is implied, if not actually stated, that intelligence reveals itself chiefly in the noegenetic mental processes which alone "are generative of new items in the field of cognition." Although there is a great deal more involved than a mere reopening of the old discussion on 'association' which many writers have accepted as

[10] Spearman: *The Nature of Intelligence and the Principles of Cognition.*

having been settled by James—for example, Spearman carries his distinctions down to the sensory and perceptual levels—it is obvious that we have here a position opposed to the reduction of all mental differences to quantitative variations in the number or strength of habitual associations.

The leading advocate of this latter position is Thorndike, who, in the interests of simplicity, continuity, and explanations which are analogous to those which are so successful in the realm of natural science, has frequently stated his preference for the belief that the differences between the 'higher' and 'lower' forms of thinking can ultimately be reduced to differences in the functioning of associative 'bonds'. The following quotation[11] will serve to illustrate his position: "Nothing . . . looks less like the mysterious operations of a faculty of reasoning transcending the laws of connection-forming than the behavior of men in response to novel situations."

Two investigations have sprung directly out of these different positions. McRae[12] took the tests in the Stanford Binet Scale and made a classification of them according as they appeared to illustrate the mental processes classified by Spearman as noegenetic or to depend on habituation or experience, such as, for example, is obtained in school life. He used sub-classes for those which more doubtfully fell into these two classifications. He then tested 161 physically defective and 244 mentally defective children between the ages of 7 and 14. The former were chosen so as to get cases which were suffering mainly from lack of schooling, while the latter group provided cases with fairly normal school attendance but ascertained mental defect. The assumption was that the most satisfactory tests of innate ability should be those in which superior natural endowment enabled the physically defective children to furthest outstrip the mentally defective despite inferior educational opportunity, while the least satisfactory tests would be those in which superior educational opportunity enabled the mentally deficient children to approach nearest to the physically defective. The percentage of each group passing each test was ascertained and the percentage difference between these figures calculated and compared with the *a priori* analysis. For example, the test of counting backward was passed by 44 per cent of the men-

[11] Thorndike: *Educational Psychology*, Vol. II, p. 47.
[12] McRae: Testing of Physically Defective and Mentally Defective Children. *The Australasian Journal of Psychology and Philosophy*, March, 1926.

tally deficient children and 77 per cent of the physically defective, the comprehension test (year 8) gave 51 per cent and 58 per cent for the two groups, while the similarities test was passed by 28 per cent and 60 per cent, respectively. Although the practical testing did not in all cases bear out the theoretical classification, it is claimed that there was a very large measure of agreement. The coefficient of association between the *a priori* and the *a posteriori* rankings for forty tests on which data were available was .89.

Tilton[13] approaches the problem of differences in types of mental process from a slightly different angle and by different methods. He takes up particularly Burt's claim (see p. 40) that the best tests of intelligence are those which involve the higher mental processes. He doubts whether Burt's work settles the matter, since here as in similar investigations stress is placed on the speed rather than on the number and extent of associations. He seeks, then, to compare the relative efficiency of tests, depending on extent of association and on higher mental processes. He chooses as his 'habit' or association tests vocabulary, information, and arithmetic habits. As 'power' tests he takes completions, analogies, arithmetic completions, and arithmetic equations. The subjects were 829 cases who are said to be a somewhat selected sample of eighth grade graduates. The intercorrelations of the scores obtained on the various tests were worked out, and it was found that the scores in the tests used to measure association correlate as highly with the power tests as the power tests do among themselves or as the habit tests do with the habit tests. Similarly, no significant differences are obtained in the correlations of the two types of test either with school success or with intelligence as judged by a rating based on score in all the tests plus school success. He sums up in his conclusions, "We find in the scores which we obtained evidence for believing that the number of correct habitual responses which a boy graduating from grammar school can make is as good an index of his intelligence as is his ability to respond adequately to more novel test situations."

SUMMING UP ON INVESTIGATIONS

An attempt to discuss adequately all or even some of the issues

[13] Tilton: *The Relation Between Association and the Higher Mental Processes.* Teachers College, Columbia University, Contributions to Education, No. 218.

raised thus far in this chapter would obviously take us far beyond the limits desirable in a book of this kind. Before presenting our own results, however, we must attempt to gain some general impression from the opinions and investigations which have been reviewed.

So far as comparisons of normal with inferior minds are concerned it does appear that there are genuine differences in their performance on different kinds of tests. There does, also, seem to be some strand of similarity running through the tests which various investigators have selected as being the most discriminative. But in all our comparisons of those of equivalent mental age but different degrees of ability (different I.Q.'s) it must be remembered that those of poorer ability have lived longer in the world and that it is possible to claim that any differences in performance are accountable for by this fact.

It appears necessary, however, to carry the analysis a step further and ask: What is the significance of the fact that mere length of experience affects some types of mental process more than others? If this fact were a little more firmly established and if it were shown that the tests which correlate most highly with ability and least with age had certain features in common, it seems to the writer that it would be at least presumptive evidence of the functioning of different types of mental process—though, perhaps, other interpretations might be given according to one's general psychological theory. If it is true that certain tests depend more on opportunity and others more on native ability (inasmuch as more capable individuals can reach a given standard at an earlier age than can less capable individuals), there would be few if any psychologists who would not prefer to give greater emphasis to the latter type in the construction of scales for the measurement of intelligence. In this connection it may be remarked that merely to cast a test into a certain form, such as 'completions', is no guarantee that we have achieved our aim of obtaining a test which depends chiefly on native ability, even if it should be found that on the whole tests of this kind do so. In the case of investigations using group tests it seems that wherever the aim is to ascertain something about the discriminative value of the type of test in question, a more minute examination of the test elements than is usually reported is desirable.

We seem to be on more difficult ground in attempting to decide whether within individuals of similar ability or within the same individual we can find evidence of the functioning of lower and higher forms of thinking. In his book describing the construction of the CAVD tests Professor Thorndike makes an interesting distinction between altitude and range in intelligence and points out the close correlation between the two. It seems to the writer that it would not be a very big step to a distinction between 'power' tests which depend largely on altitude and 'habit' tests which depend more on range at a given altitude. It may be that the correlation between altitude and range is much higher when we limit ourselves to individuals with a given altitude than when we include a wider range of altitudes, and that the correlations within a given altitude become higher as we move to higher altitudes. It may be facts of this kind which make it difficult to discover evidence of the existence of different types of mental process within the same individual or among a group of individuals of homogeneous ability. Whether high correlations in this matter are themselves regarded as evidence of the absence of any fundamental distinctions between types of mental process will depend upon one's initial views in the matter and one's interpretation of the meaning of correlation.

CHAPTER VI

COMPARISON OF NORMAL CHILDREN WITH IMBECILES

The investigation here being reported involves a bigger discrepancy between the ability, and hence between the chronological ages, of the two groups than most of the investigations referred to in the previous chapter. Hence the chief facts to be brought out in a comparison of the performance of the two groups will relate to the attempt to find out in general what the effect is of the greater experience of the older group in causing differences in test performance. We have in the scale as it stands a wide collection of tasks which for adult intelligence at low levels are placed in groups of fairly uniform difficulty. By examining our results we can find out which of these tasks have for children a significantly different degree of difficulty. It must of course be remembered that our chances of finding differences by this method are necessarily more limited than they would be if we also tried adults of poor ability on a wide range of tests found to be of suitable degrees of difficulty for normal children of equivalent mental age.

In our presentation of results up to this point we have been chiefly concerned with the capacity of the CAVD Test in general to rank the children who were tested and the extent to which the various levels represented steady increments of difficulty for them. We found nothing here which would clearly demonstrate differences in the performance of the two groups.

There are, however, certain implicit comparisons in the results which we obtained in Chapter III from an examination of the behavior of the separate tests in the scale. If a graph for the adults were available corresponding to Figure 4, we would find a much greater degree of coincidence in the lines representing the scores on each test because the scale was so arranged that the four types of test contributed about equally to the total score on each level. Since the vocabulary test has such a markedly smaller range for the children than have any of the other tests, it would seem to be a reasonable inference to suppose that of the four tests in the scale this is the one which is the most heavily weighted for experience.

CAVD SCORES FOR EQUIVALENT MENTAL AGES

Since there was available a table giving for the imbeciles the CAVD scores obtained by those with given mental ages, it will be worth while to compare the scores obtained by our younger subjects for equivalent mental ages. Will the scores of the two groups correspond absolutely at one or more parts of the mental age range and will the increase in score per unit of mental age in one group bear any constant relation to the increase in the other group? The results are given in Table V. For the purposes of this table we have picked out points six months apart in the mental age range lying between three years and six years and give for each the average CAVD score for the two groups. In the fourth column is given the difference between the scores of the two groups for each mental age. It will at once be noticed that the score of the normal children of three years mental age is higher than the score of the imbeciles of equal mental age, but that when we come to the six-year mental age group the position is quite reversed, the children being easily surpassed by the adults. In between the two ends of the table we have a strikingly steady change over from one situation to the other, with the crossing taking place somewhere about the mental age of four.

TABLE V

CAVD SCORES OF THE TWO GROUPS AT EQUIVALENT MENTAL AGES

MENTAL AGE	CAVD Scores		Difference
	Imbeciles	Normal Children	
6.0	158	140	−18
5.6	136	127	− 9
5.0	115	109	− 6
4.6	93	89	− 4
4.0	71	69	− 2
3.6	50	54	+ 4
3.0	28	40	+12

It is extremely interesting to speculate as to what the interpretation of this table should be. It might be possible to argue that the imbeciles at low mental ages are penalized as compared with children, through lack of ability to do themselves justice in test situations; but, if anything, the argument is probably the other way. In any case arguments of this kind would have little force except at the lowest levels. It must be remembered that we really have here a comparison of performance on two types of mental test with performance on the Binet Test constant for each group. It is reasonable to suppose that the CAVD is more heavily weighted for experience than is the Binet. If this is granted, it seems possible to explain the variations in CAVD score by reference to two coöperating factors, viz., length of experience and ability to profit by it. With adults of very inferior intelligence their twenty or thirty years of experience have not been worth as much to them (in terms of CAVD) as have three years or so been to bright or normal children. With increasing ability the advantage which the adult group have on the CAVD Test becomes greater and greater owing to the fact that they have been able to profit more from experience. It would appear that this is at least as reasonable an explanation as any other. It would be interesting if further investigation should confirm the idea that a mental age of about four years is the level at which length of experience and ability to profit by it counterbalance each other. It would provide a crucial point for the carrying out of various experiments.

This point has been referred to by Taylor,[1] though her estimate places the age a great deal higher than four. She says, "The older individuals tended to pass more of the tests influenced by mere maturity. As a matter of fact six and seven years mental age is about the same for the various chronological ages. The similarities far outweigh the differences."

We would have to modify somewhat the inferences suggested above if it were found that the differences in CAVD score were due almost entirely to the different performances of the two groups on one only of the tests in the scale—let us suppose the vocabulary test. We have not the data which would enable us to analyze this question, but on the whole the chances are that the differences are contributed to by all four tests.

[1] Taylor: *An Inventory of the Minds of Six and Seven Years Mental Age.* Teachers College, Columbia University, Contributions to Education, No. 134.

COMPARISON OF PERCENTAGES OF SUCCESSES

Most of the remainder of this study is based on tables which were available giving for the imbeciles the percentage of successes on each level and on each item in each level for the tasks in completions, arithmetic, vocabulary and directions. These percentages were based on results obtained with two groups of imbeciles, one of one hundred and the other of eighty individuals. The percentages of successes for the two groups are given separately, and we shall make use later of the differences between them, but in the meantime it will be simpler and quite satisfactory for our purpose to work with the average of the percentages obtained by the two groups. The groups of imbeciles had mental ages ranging from two to five years. We do not know the performance for finer subdivisions of mental age.

In order to make comparisons, we have selected one hundred cases of normal children and have ascertained the corresponding percentage of successes in each item in their case. In making this selection we have sought to limit our cases to the same mental age range, viz., two to five years. This has meant the omission of some of our brightest children. At the same time, in order to avoid the inclusion of any of inferior mentality, we have eliminated those whose scores fell into the lowest quartile for each age group. We are thus comparing the performance of a group of imbeciles with that of a group of children lying within the same range of mental age but without any more precise knowledge of the manner in which the two groups are distributed. Since the average mental age of one of the groups may be higher than the other, we must be cautious in making absolute comparisons; we can without such caution compare the relative performance on different levels or on different items within each level.

In Table VI we give for each group the percentage of cases passing 50 per cent or more of the items at each level. Thus, taking each level in each test with its ten tasks as the unit and defining success as one-half or more of the items in each unit correct, we see that Level A in Completions was passed by 83 per cent of the imbeciles and 96 per cent of the children, and so on for the other levels.

In Table VII we have the same facts from a slightly different

TABLE VI

COMPARISON OF PERCENTAGES SUCCEEDING ON EACH LEVEL

	LEVEL	IMBECILE PER CENT	NORMAL PER CENT
Completions	A	83	96
	B	60½	58
	C	31	39
	D	1½	3
Arithmetic	A	74½	79
	B	47	59
	C	18	24
	D	5	3
Directions	A	88	100
	B	56	79
	C	23	59
	D	13	33
Vocabulary	A	80½	99
	B	53	79
	C	16½	13
	D	3	4

TABLE VII

COMPARISON OF THE MEAN PERCENTAGES OBTAINED ON EACH LEVEL

	LEVEL	IMBECILE PER CENT	NORMAL PER CENT
Completions	A	73.5	80.9
	B	50.9	51.6
	C	30.5	30.2
	D	13.4	7.5
Arithmetic	A	65.5	75.2
	B	45.4	55.2
	C	23.0	29.2
	D	13.8	8.8
Directions	A	77.9	86.5
	B	52.3	68.8
	C	25.7	47.3
	D	16.5	31.8
Vocabulary	A	75.6	82.6
	B	48.4	61.0
	C	25.2	26.9
	D	11.7	12.9

point of view and thus may discuss the two tables together. Table VII is obtained by calculating for each group the mean of the percentages of successes on each item in each of the levels. Thus for the imbecile group the percentage of subjects passing each item on Level A in Completions varied round 73.5, while for the other group it varied round 80.9.

It will be noticed in these tables that there is a tendency for the normal percentages in all tests to be higher on the earlier levels. In the upper levels there is a tendency for the imbeciles to reduce this advantage, if not actually to pass the percentage obtained by the children. This, however, is not true of the directions test (cf. Figure 4), where the children consistently do better throughout. This tendency of the imbeciles to gain on the upper levels is possibly a reflection of the fact already suggested that the dull who score on higher levels are of higher mental age and have on this account benefited more from their experience. In this connection it is interesting to notice that the directions test, in which the children maintain their advantage, is the one which contains least in the way of informational elements.

CHAPTER VII

COMPARISON OF PERFORMANCE ON INDIVIDUAL ITEMS

We now turn finally to the question of the comparative performance of the two groups on the individual items in the scale. The object of this minute examination is to ascertain which, if any, of the tests are markedly different in difficulty for the two groups, to see which of the two groups has the advantage in such cases, and to see if, perhaps, there is some common characteristic running through the tests which thus stand out.

The method which has been employed is to calculate the standard error of the difference between the proportions (in this case, the percentages) of successes obtained by the two groups. We have then found the ratio of this standard error to the observed difference. The formula for this standard error is given by Yule [1] in two forms. The first, $\epsilon_{12}^2 = p_0 q_0 \left(\dfrac{1}{n_1} + \dfrac{1}{n_2} \right)$, is for use where the two universes are regarded as similar, in order to see whether the difference between the two proportions may have arisen merely as a fluctuation of simple sampling; the second, $\epsilon_{12}^2 = \dfrac{p_1 q_1}{n_1} + \dfrac{p_2 q_2}{n_2}$, is for use where the assumption is that the universes are different, in order to see whether if we took fresh samples in the same way we might through errors of sampling fail to get any differences in the observed proportions.

Our primary interest is to compare the proportion of successes as between the children and the imbeciles, but for purposes of comparison we have computed the standard error of the difference between the percentages of the two imbecile groups. The fourth column in Tables VIII–XI gives the ratio of the observed difference to the standard error of the difference between the imbecile groups when the standard error is calculated by the first formula above. The last column gives the corresponding ratio for the normal and subnormal groups when the standard error is based on the second formula. For example,

[1] Yule: *An Introduction to the Theory of Statistics.* p. 269.

TABLE VIII

PERCENTAGES OF SUCCESSES IN INDIVIDUAL ITEMS OF COMPLETIONS TEST

LEVEL		IMBECILES		OBS. DIFFCE. S.E. OF DIFF.	MEAN IMBECILE	NORMAL	OBS. DIFFCE. S.E. OF DIFF.	
		100	80					
A	1	78	84	1.4	81	95	3.8	
	2	77	79	.3	78	97	5.4	
	3	78	81	.5	79	94	3.9	
	2	82	81	.2	81	92	2.8	
	5	68	72½	.6	70	78	1.5	
	6	59	71	1.7	65	82	3.2	
	7	69	74	.7	72	93	5.0	
	8	67	62½	.6	65	74	1.6	
	9	63	66	.4	65	35		5.1
	10	81	73	1.2	77	69		1.4
B	1	46	56	1.3	51	49		.3
	2	65	56	1.4	61	64	.5	
	3	57	38	2.5	48	62	2.3	
	4	56	55	.1	56	48		1.3
	5	53	50	.4	52	64	2.0	
	6	50	45	.6	48	55	1.1	
	7	56	45	1.4	51	39		2.0
	8	51	49	.3	50	48		.3
	9	48	56	1.1	52	60	1.3	
	10	40	39	.1	40	27		2.3
C	1	26	26	0	26	31	.9	
	2	37	30	.4	34	38	.7	
	3	34	35	.1	35	23		2.1
	4	44	34	1.4	39	24		2.7
	5	36	32½	.5	34	31		.6
	6	37	31	.8	34	43	1.4	
	7	27	26	.1	27	15		2.5
	8	31	22½	1.2	27	44	2.9	
	9	30	27½	.4	29	37	1.4	
	10	22	17½	.7	20	16		.8
D	1	35			35	9		5.6
	2	17	19	.3	18	5		3.6
	3	12			12	13	.1	
	4	19	15	.7	17	4		3.8
	5	2			2	0		
	6	2	6	1.4	4	3		.4
	7	9	4	1.4	6	15	2.3	
	8	1	2½	.3	2	11	2.7	
	9	13	14	.2	13			
	10	11	1	2.6	6			

Note. In this and the following tables the ratios which appear on the left of the last column represent the cases in which the percentage of successes of the children was greater than the percentage for the imbeciles. Conversely the cases on the right of the column represent tests which were more difficult for the children than for the imbeciles.

TABLE IX

PERCENTAGES OF SUCCESSES IN INDIVIDUAL ITEMS OF THE ARITHMETIC TEST

LEVEL		IMBECILES		OBS. DIFFCE. $\frac{\text{S.E. of}}{\text{Diff.}}$	MEAN IMBECILE	NORMAL	OBS. DIFFCE. $\frac{\text{S.E. of}}{\text{Diff.}}$
		100	80				
A	1	67	64	.4	65	74	1.4
	2	53	57½	.6	55	65	1.6
	3	75	73	.3	74	71	.5
	4	56	67½	1.6	61	61	
	5	67	65	.3	66	67	.1
	6	64	73	1.4	68	94	6.1
	7	67	72½	.8	69	96	6.9
	8	61	67½	.9	64	90	5.6
	9	72	64	1.2	68	68	
	10	60	71	1.5	65	66	.1
B	1	28	50	3.0	39	61	3.6
	2	55	46	1.2	50	52	.1
	3	49	42	.9	45	37	1.3
	4	49	44	.7	46	94	10.9
	5	40	54	1.9	47	60	2.1
	6	55	51	.5	53	54	.1
	7	42	42½	.1	42	50	.6
	8	27	49	3.0	38	44	.5
	9	44	49	.7	46	49	.3
	10	57	40	2.3	48	51	.3
C	1	26	24	.3	25	23	.3
	2	20	24	.6	22	16	.9
	3	30	24	.9	29	27	.2
	4	23	29	.9	26	83	11.6
	5	38	17	3.1	27	26	.1
	6	9	20	2.1	14	18	.5
	7	16	30	2.2	23	35	2.0
	8	21	32	1.7	26	23	.6
	9	15	22	1.2	18	19	.1
	10	21	19	.3	20	22	.3
D	1	24	5	3.6	14	3	3.5
	2	18	16	.4	17	10	1.7
	3	11	10	.2	10	10	
	4	11	11	0	11	19	1.7
	5	13	14	.2	13	8	1.3
	6	23	11	2.1	17	4	3.8
	7	22	14	1.4	18	15	3.6
	8	12	12	0	12	7	1.4
	9	21	10	2.1	15	5	2.9
	10	17	5	2.5	11	7	1.3

See Note to Table VIII

TABLE X

PERCENTAGES OF SUCCESSES IN INDIVIDUAL ITEMS OF THE VOCABULARY TEST

LEVEL	IMBECILES		OBS. DIFFCE. $\frac{\text{S.E. OF}}{\text{DIFF.}}$	MEAN IMBECILE	NORMAL	OBS. DIFFCE. $\frac{\text{S.E. OF}}{\text{DIFF.}}$
	100	80				
A 1	76	81	.8	78	54	4.1
2	71	79	1.2	75	100	8.1
3	74	75	.1	74	84	2.0
4	76	80	.6	78	88	2.3
5	76	89	2.2	82	78	.8
6	73	85	2.0	79	89	2.3
7	72	73	.1	72	61	1.8
8	72	79	1.0	75	89	3.2
9	67	77½	1.5	72	85	2.6
10	67	76	1.3	71	98	5.4
B 1	48	55	.9	51	80	5.4
2	49	52½	.5	50	66	2.8
3	51	61	1.3	56	67	1.8
4	46	62½	2.2	54	70	2.7
5	44	42½	.2	43	38	.8
6	47	54	.9	50	73	4.0
7	40	36	.5	38	16	4.3
8	43	50	.9	46	88	8.6
9	41	57½	2.2	49	66	2.9
10	39	56	2.3	47	46	.1
C 1	26	36	1.4	31	33	.2
2	25	15	1.6	20	9	2.6
3	24	31	1.0	27	38	2.5
4	24	49	3.4	36	25	2.2
5	23	19	.6	21	42	3.8
6	22	22½	.1	22	11	2.6
7	21	30	1.2	25	33	1.4
8	20	24	.6	22	25	.3
9	21	25	.6	23	48	4.1
10	21	30	1.2	25	5	3.3
D 1	12	21	1.6	16	17	.1
2	15	9	.8	12	8	1.2
3	11	9	.4	10	23	2.8
4	14	16	.3	15	17	.3
5	15	12½	.6	14	3	3.5
6	9	12½	.7	11	20	1.8
7	14	17½	.6	16	16	
8	9	7½	.6	8	11	.8
9	6	8	.5	7	8	.2
10	4	12½	2.1	8	6	.7

See Note to Table VIII

TABLE XI

PERCENTAGES OF SUCCESSES IN INDIVIDUAL ITEMS OF DIRECTIONS TEST

LEVEL		IMBECILES		OBS. DIFFCE. S.E. OF DIFF.	MEAN IMBECILE	NORMAL	OBS. DIFFCE. S.E. OF DIFF.
		100	80				
A	1	83	87½	.7	85	99	5.0
	2	85	84	.2	84	96	3.8
	3	65	69	.5	67	84	3.4
	4	80	80	0	80	34	8.2
	5	81	86	.8	83	95	3.8
	6	85	84	.2	84	89	1.2
	7	72	70	.3	71	93	5.2
	8	80	86	1.0	83	98	4.8
	9	73	75	.3	74	90	3.6
	10	63	73	1.5	68	87	3.9
B	1	59	65	.8	62	68	1.0
	2	43	57½	1.9	50	68	3.0
	3	58	66	1.1	62	80	3.3
	4	47	50	.4	48	68	3.1
	5	40	44	.5	42	54	1.9
	6	43	75	4.4	59	71	2.1
	7	49	44	.7	46	56	1.7
	8	42	59	2.3	50	82	6.0
	9	40	76	4.6	57	79	4.0
	10		47½	.	47	42	.8
C	1	35	34	.1	34	67	5.6
	2	24	29	.7	26	59	5.6
	3	27	36	1.3	31	48	2.8
	4	17	32½	2.4	24	38	2.2
	5	23	19	.6	21	43	3.8
	6	19	27½	1.3	23	42	3.3
	7	20	22½	.4	21	55	5.8
	8	30	35	.7	32	40	1.3
	9	20	24	.6	22	35	2.1
	10	22	25	.5	23	46	4.0
D	1	16	26	1.6	21	39	3.1
	2	8	10	.5	9	18	2.0
	3	16	25	1.5	20	26	.9
	4	10	16	1.2	13	34	3.9
	5	16	24	1.3	20	37	3.0
	6	8	22½	2.7	15	27	2.3
	7	13	30	2.9	21	40	3.2
	8	14	17½	.6	16	11	1.2
	9	16	17½	.2	17	52	6.1
	10	22	9	2.4	15	34	3.5

See Note to Table VIII

in item 1 of Level A in the completions test the actual difference
in the percentage of successes gained by the two imbecile groups
is 1.4 times the standard error of the difference; whereas on the
same item the difference which was obtained between the percentage of successes gained by the children and the mean percentage of the imbecile groups is 3.8 times the standard error
of the difference. The interpretation of these ratios depends on
the fact that any difference which is more than three times the
standard error is very unlikely to have occurred as the result of
simple sampling. In the case just quoted we are not at all sure
that the difference of six per cent between the successes of the two
imbecile groups would not entirely disappear if two other groups
were taken from the same population; but the difference of four-
teen per cent between the successes of normals and imbeciles on
the same item, since it is nearly four times the standard error of
the difference, is undoubtedly a reflection of a genuine difference
of difficulty which would be maintained by any representative
sampling from the two populations. We can thus infer that this
item is significantly easier for children than for subnormal adults.[2]

The ratios which occur in the last column of the tables are a
reflection of two types of difference between the performance of
the two groups. The ratios will be high when the test or the level
as a whole is much easier for one of the groups than for the other.
This will be indicated by a tendency for uniformly high ratios to
occur. On the other hand, when the ratio for a particular item
stands much above the other ratios for the test or the level concerned, it shows that that particular item differs significantly in
difficulty for the two groups. We are interested in both forms
of comparison, but since some of the facts we have already discussed spring from displacement in the general difficulty of the
levels (see Tables VI and VII) we shall here concentrate our
attention on any individual items which stand out. From this
point of view a ratio will have to be somewhat higher to stand
out when it occurs among other high ratios.

We must also notice carefully the group for which the item is
easier. In this connection a high ratio will be all the more significant when it depends upon a difference which varies in direction

---

[2] In the calculation of p_n in formula 1 we have allowed ourselves the approximation of
using the unweighted instead of the weighted mean. Since the numbers in the two
groups are not widely different, this approximation gives us results quite sufficiently
accurate for our comparisons.

from most of the other differences in the level. We have a striking example in the directions test, where although only three items in the whole test are easier for the imbeciles one of these has a ratio of 8.2 times the standard error.

We are now in a position to select for discussion the outstanding items. We shall on the basis of the considerations just dis-

TABLE XII

CLASSIFICATION OF ITEMS DIFFERING IN DIFFICULTY FOR THE GROUPS

	A. EASIER FOR CHILDREN				B. EASIER FOR IMBECILES		
	Cases in which differences are probably significant	Significant	Outstanding		Cases in which differences are probably significant	Significant	Outstanding
Completions	A 1￼ A 3￼ A 6￼ C 8￼ D 8	A 2￼ A 7		Completions	C 4	A 9￼ D 1￼ D 2￼ D 4	
Arithmetic	B 1	A 8	A6￼ A7￼ B4￼ C4	Arithmetic	D9	D 1￼ D 6￼ D 7	
Vocabulary	A 9￼ B 2￼ B 4￼ B 9￼ D 3	A10￼ B 1￼ B 6￼ C 5	A2￼ B8	Vocabulary		A 1￼ B 7￼ C10￼ D 5	
Directions	A 2￼ A 5￼ A10￼ C 5￼ D 4	A 1￼ A 7￼ A 8￼ B 9￼ C 1￼ C 2￼ C 7￼ C10	B8￼ D9	Directions			A4

cussed attempt to distinguish between those items in which the difference is probably significant, marked, or striking. Obviously the classification is to some extent an arbitrary one. In Table XII we have given the items by reference to level and number and give below the nature of these items in detail.

The tests referred to by letter and number in Table XII are as follows:

COMPLETIONS

A1 You are sitting on a ......
A3 At night you sleep in ......
A6 Mary has a ring on her ......
C8 We see with our ......
D8 Horses are big and ......
A2 We take a ride on the ......
A7 You wear gloves on your ......

C4 The ...... is barking at the cat.
A9 We go to church on ......
D1 Boys ...... baseball.
D2 The stars and the ...... will shine tonight.
D4 A boy has ...... and legs.

ARITHMETIC

B1 Counting of two pennies. (3 of 3 trials correct)
A8 Showing the biggest of three squares. (2 of 3 trials correct)
A6 Showing the smallest of three pencils. (2 of 3)
A7 Showing the smallest of three squares. (2 of 3)
B4 Showing the biggest pile of pennies. (13 in one, 2 in other, 3 of 3)
C4 Showing the biggest pile of pennies. (10 in one, 5 in other, 3 of 3)

D9 Adds unseen 3 plus 2. (2 of 3)
D1 Counts 15 pennies. (3 of 3)
D6 Names 5 fingers when shown. (5 of 5)
D7 Answers 'Which is biggest, 3 or 1?' (2 of 3)

VOCABULARY

We give first the name of the object which the child was asked to indicate, and following this the names of the other objects of which pictures were shown at the same time.

A9 Socks ....trousers, suspenders, shoe, foot
B2 Bag ....cask, bread, corn, infant
B4 Wings ....fish-bowl, paper, fish, house
B9 Cradle ....chicken, bird, rattle, rooster
D3 Screw ....hammer, nail, wrench, nut
A10 Dog ....girl, table, boy, chair
B1 Soup ....spoon, meat, fork, cup

B6 Comb ....hair, toothbrush, mouth, eye
C5 Puppy ....dog, lamb, ram, meat
A2 Man ....bed, door, horse, window
B8 Door ....bed, horse, man, window

A1 Pitcher ....milk bottle, vase, cup, cow
B7 Locomotive ......dress, house, sun, tree
C10 Kennel ....dog, bees, hive, insect
D5 Cartridge ....gun, rifle, military tank, soldier

DIRECTIONS

A2 Make a line like this. (Making before subject straight line of 2 inches)
A5 Put the cover on the box.
A10 Make a ring. (Having shown how some minutes before)
C5 Make a ring and a cross. (Having previously been shown how)
D4 See the ring? Make 2 crosses in the ring.
A1 Make a ring like this.
A7 Put the pennies in the box and then shake the box.
A8 Stand on that paper.
B9 Make the other leg on this man. (Complete model and incomplete drawing)
C1 See the square? Make a ring in the square.
C2 Now make another ring in the square.
C7 Draw a line to finish the square. (Three sides of square shown)
C10 Make two squares out of these. (Two similarly incomplete squares shown)
B8 Make the other arm on this man.
D9 Make this a circle. (Incomplete circle shown)

A4 You can write, can't you? Show me how you can write.

DISCUSSION OF RESULTS OF STUDY OF DIFFERENCES IN INDIVIDUAL ITEMS

We must now attempt to indicate any general tendencies which are revealed by the foregoing analysis. We shall treat each of the tests separately.

Completions Test. In this test it is worth noting that with one exception the tests which are easier for the imbeciles have the omissions within the sentence instead of at the end of it; whereas all the tests which are easier for the children have the last word omitted. With the possible exception of tests A9, D1, and D2 one cannot suspect that the tests on which the adults do best favor them on informational grounds; therefore it seems to be a reasonable inference that for the examples in the test the form in which they are cast has a great deal to do with the relative difficulty for the two groups. It is unfortunate that results on Level E were not available for the adults, inasmuch as the example which in that level stood out as easiest for the children (E7: Snow is white, coal is......) appears to depend very directly on apprehension of a suggested relationship.

Arithmetic Test. The arithmetic test gives us the clearest cut and some of the most decisive differences of all. With one exception all the items on which the children surpassed the adults relate to the discrimination of the size of presented objects. These tests were relatively so much easier for the children that they must depend on mental processes in which the two groups differ characteristically. Apparently the presentation of an object and a verbal term expressing a relationship of size is far more apt to educe the correct response in the case of normal than in the case of very inferior mentality. It may be that the difficulty for the adults lies in the apprehension of the terms 'longest,' 'biggest,' and so on; but in any case the fact that their much more frequent opportunities of hearing and appreciating the meaning of such terms have not resulted in a better grasp of their significance supports rather than modifies the inference suggested above. The fact that the children surpass the adults in counting two pennies three times out of three a great deal more than they do in counting them two times out of three may be possibly explained on the supposition that if the children can count at all they can do it more consistently than the adults. In general the adults stand well ahead on the counting tests.

Vocabulary Test. The vocabulary test results must be interpreted in the light of the discussion given in Chapter III. An inspection of the words which were found easier for the children will show that most of them come well within the range of the child's experience. This is probably not true of the words which were easier for the adults.

Directions Test. There are some definite suggestions to be obtained from examining the examples in the directions test which are easier for the children. Perhaps the one most noticeable is that all the directions tests which require a completion of some kind occur in the list of those on which the children did better. The tests are: the supplying of the other leg, the supplying of the other arm, the completion of the three-sided square, the completion of the two three-sided squares, and the completion of the circle. Apparently an incomplete drawing more readily suggests its completion in the case of normal than in the case of subnormal intelligence. One young child who caught sight by accident of the incomplete square before her testing had brought her to it remarked, "I want to fill that up."

The test involving an imitation of writing was the one instance in the directions test where the adults had a decided advantage over the children. The child's response was usually to draw something or to make marks which even by a liberal interpretation could not be regarded as resembling letters.

If any one general inference from these results is possible, it would seem to be that the tests involving an appreciation of relative size and those involving an appreciation of relationship of given to incomplete parts are characteristically easier for the group representing normal intelligence.

CHAPTER VIII

SUMMARY

We give in conclusion the points which have been discussed in this study and the inferences which have been suggested by it.

1. We have discussed the significance of scales which provide a series of tasks of graded difficulty in given functions.

2. The CAVD Test is such a scale based on the performances of those of mature intelligence.

3. The present investigation provides a comparison between the performances on this test of a group of imbeciles and a group of normal children of equivalent mental ages.

4. The correlation between CAVD and Binet Tests was .92 for the group of cases where both tests were applied.

5. On the whole the CAVD Test was found to be quite as attractive for young children as a test of this type could be expected to be.

6. We have seen that the early levels of the CAVD Test give steadily rising scores for successive chronological age groups and steadily decreasing scores for any one group on successively higher levels. In other words, the test as applied to children does not reveal any radical alterations in the difficulty of the levels considered as units.

7. There is a great deal of interest in the study of the development of the abilities involved in the separate tests of the scale and in a discussion of the nature of the abilities required by each test.

8. A vocabulary test in picture form is not necessarily easier than a test in oral form using the same words.

9. Our age scales for the measurement of intelligence cannot give us information as to the relative rate of the development of intelligence from one year to another.

10. When we plot the increments in CAVD score made by successive mental age groups, we get on the whole a fairly constant increment over the ages for which we have results. There is no suggestion of a decrease in the rate of growth for the ages in question.

11. We have discussed the various opinions which are held as to the nature of the differences between normal and inferior minds and have seen the relation of this question to the possibility of distinguishing between higher and lower mental processes. Some of the chief investigations relating to these questions are reviewed.

12. In connection with the above questions we discuss the nature of the concept of mental age.

13. From a comparison of the performance of children with imbeciles one of the most interesting results obtained arose from ascertaining the CAVD scores for those of equivalent mental ages in the two groups. We found that at younger mental ages the children surpass the adults but that at the higher mental ages the opposite is true. We suggested a possible explanation of this which, if correct, throws an interesting light on the relationship of degree of intelligence to ability to profit from experience.

14. An examination of the percentages of successes on the different levels of each test shows a tendency for the children to surpass the adults more at the earlier than at the higher levels in completions, arithmetic, and vocabulary, but to maintain their advantage through all levels in directions.

15. A detailed study of the individual items shows that some of these stand out very distinctly in their relative difficulty for the two groups. We have classified these and attempted to ascertain any common features among those items which stand out as distinctly easier for one or the other of the two groups.

REVIEW OF MAIN ISSUES

It would appear that a scale for the measurement of intelligence based on the performance of adults of very inferior ability may be strikingly successful in its grading of young children of equivalent mental ages when judged by its correlation with the Binet Test, by the performance of successive age groups, and by the performance of individuals and groups on successive levels of the test.

Bearing of Results on Test Construction and Interpretation. The foregoing statement does not, however, mean that we can without hesitation directly compare scores made by groups with extreme C.A. differences. We have found that in terms of absolute performance there are, for given Binet mental ages, noticeable differences between the two groups and that these differences vary both in amount and in direction for different mental ages. Our results suggest (see Table V) that children with a Binet mental age of, say, 6 years tend to be penalized by the CAVD Test if we wish to compare them with adults of equivalent Binet scores. If we are judging intelligence from CAVD alone, this would mean that we would tend to underestimate the ability of these children should we accept the Binet Test as a criterion and, in our prediction of Binet M.A. from CAVD score, use the regression line based on adult performances. The table mentioned suggests, however, that children as compared with adults are not necessarily penalized on a scale of this kind. At mental ages at about three, if the comparison and interpretation are carried out on the same assumptions, we will tend to overestimate the ability of the children. The matter is complicated by the consideration that in accepting the Binet Test as a criterion we are accepting the result of applying to adults a test that was standardized on the performance of children.

Should we test the 'old dull' by the 'young bright' and *vice versa?* Our own results and some of the investigations reported demonstrate clearly enough that there may be significant differences in the difficulty of a task for two groups of different chronological ages but, so far as we can judge, equivalent mental ages. In general, then, our investigation would appear to support those who claim that individuals should be tested by comparison with the performance of those close to their own chronological age. We feel, however, that it is impossible to force a definite 'yes' or 'no' answer to the question at the head of this paragraph. It might, for example, be more legitimate to apply to adults a test based on the performance of children (as when we apply the Binet Test to adults of low I.Q.) than to apply to children a scale based on adult performances (as in the present investigation).

It is suggested by our results that the purpose for which we wish to use our test scores also has some bearing on the legitimacy of the procedure we are discussing. If we wish to use them merely to arrange in the order of their intellectual ability the cases included in a fairly homogeneous C.A. group, it may be that our use of a test standardized on a different C.A. group is more valid than it would be if we used these results to judge the standing of a group or individual in terms of some concept of intelligence (such as 'mental age') which is assumed to stand for a constant quantity no matter what the C.A. may be.

Again, if we run the risk of making general the interpretation we have given to Table V, it could be claimed that at some mental levels there is a greater chance than at other mental levels of getting misleading results through the application of a test based on a widely different C.A. group. Thus if we make the statement that differences in length of experience are apt to affect the relative difficulty of given tests for two groups different in C.A. but similar in general intellectual level, it may be necessary to qualify this statement not only for the amount of C.A. difference but also for the mental level which we have in mind.

Finally, it appears fairly certain from our results and those of others that the answer which we give to the question before us (the question of the extent to which we are justified in using the same test for different C.A. groups) will have to be modified according to the particular combination of tests, the particular type of test, or the particular test item which we propose to apply to the two C.A. groups. It might, to take a hypothetical case, be found to be more justifiable to test both groups by the same 'opposites' test than by the same 'information' test.

It is reasonable to assume that difficulties of the kind we are discussing increase with increasing differences between the ages of the two groups. Since in our investigation the age differences are very marked, and since the discrepancy between the performance of the two groups on the scale as a whole is not very extreme, one is justified in doubting whether for the construction and application of our scales it is necessary to confine ourselves to very narrow limits of chronological age. There is, for example, so much similarity between the things which the bright child of six and the average child of eight know and are interested in that the result of the two years' longer experience which the latter has had does not appear likely to have any significant effect on any test which might be applied to the two.

The statement of test results in terms of mental age depends on the assumption that we are justified in applying the same test to individuals of different chronological ages. What we are suggesting is that the assumption is more likely to be justified for narrow than for wide chronological age differences.

Comparison of Mental Processes of Those of Normal and of Inferior Ability. We have examined the tests where there are the most outstanding differences in difficulty for the two groups in order to see whether we can find any evidence of psychological elements common to the tests which most clearly differentiate between the two groups. If we do find such evidence the assumption is that the tests in question depend on psychological processes which are more readily carried out by those of normal than by those of inferior mentality, or *vice versa.*

We become involved at this point in the difficult matter of attempting to interpret tests in the light of certain general psychological processes on which they depend. Our results are not so self-evident that they can be used to justify dogmatic statements, but we have ventured to interpret them as suggesting characteristic differences in the mental processes of the two groups. For the majority of the tests which were easier for those of inferior ability, it seems legitimate to attribute the superiority to the effect of greater length of experience; while a number of the tests which were easier for those of normal intelligence—a group including almost all those tests which were outstandingly easier— appear to have in common the appreciation and, in cases, the manipulation of spatial relationships. It would be interesting to see whether this impression would be confirmed if the same comparison were made on similar groups with a test involving logical relationships, such as a test of the ability to give opposites.

APPENDIX[1]

SAMPLES OF TESTS IN LEVELS A TO E OF CAVD SCALE

LEVEL A

COMPLETIONS

    1. 'You are sitting on a ......'
    4. 'You like to drink ......'
    10. 'You wear a ...... on your head.'

ARITHMETIC

    5. Recognizes 2 fingers. (3 of 5 trials, in given series.)
    7. Shows the biggest of three squares.
    9. Adds unseen, 1 plus 1.

VOCABULARY

(In a group of five pictures the subject is asked to point to the one underlined in the following examples):
    2. Bed, door, horse, man, window.
    4. Apple, cup, clock, hat, box.
    7. Girl, table, boy, chair, dog.

DIRECTIONS

    1. 'Make a ring like this.'
    2. 'Put the cover on the box.'
    9. 'Put your hands behind you.'

LEVEL B

COMPLETIONS

    2. 'We cut meat with a ......'
    3. 'When we are sick we call the ......'
    9. 'Apples are to ......'

ARITHMETIC

    3. 'One and one make ...... what?'
    7. 'Which is the biggest, a baby or a man?'
    9. Subtracts unseen, 3 minus 2.

VOCABULARY

    2. Cask, bread, bag, corn, baby.
    5. Letter, envelope, coins, papers, stamps.
    6. Comb, hair, brush, teeth, eye.

[1] Copies of the CAVD Test may be obtained from the Bureau of Publications, Teachers College, Columbia University, New York City.

DIRECTIONS

  2. 'Make a cross.' (Having been shown in Level A.)
  3. 'Turn the paper over on the other side.'
  10. 'Make two lines like these two.'

LEVEL C

COMPLETIONS

  1. 'Clouds are in the ......'
  4. 'The ...... is barking at the cat.'
  9. 'Roses and daisies are ......'

ARITHMETIC

  2. Counts 10 pennies. (2 of 3 trials.)
  6. 'Two and one make ...... what?'
  10. Subtracts unseen, 2 minus 2.

VOCABULARY

  5. Puppy, dog, lamb, ram, meat.
  6. Sabre, rifle, knife, cartridge, pistol.
  7. Pitcher, milk bottle, vase, cup, cow.

DIRECTIONS

  1. 'See the square? Make a ring in the square.'
  4. 'See the cup? Draw a line around the cup.' (A cup, two squares and two lines presented.)
  5. 'Make a ring and a cross up here.'

LEVEL D

COMPLETIONS

  2. 'The stars and the ...... will shine tonight.'
  6. 'Men are ...... than boys.'
  7. 'The ...... pulls the cart.'

ARITHMETIC

  1. Counts 15 pennies. (3 of 3 trials.)
  2. 'How many fingers have you on one hand?'
  3. Adds unseen, 3 plus 2. (2 of 3 trials.)

VOCABULARY

  1. Tools, screws, boys, table, nails.
  6. Trumpet, eye, mouth, ear, violin.
  10. Bow, arrow, mortar, cannon balls, aeroplane.

DIRECTIONS

  1. 'Make a cross inside the little square.' (2 squares, boy and cow.)
  4. 'See the ring? Make two crosses in the ring.'
  6. 'Draw a line around the big hand.' (3 squares and 2 hands.)

LEVEL E

COMPLETIONS

> 2. 'Horses are big ...... strong.'
> 4. 'He went to church ...... me.'
> 5. 'Most birds build their ...... in trees.'

ARITHMETIC

> 2. 'Give me half the pennies.'   (6 shown, 2 of 3 trials.)
> 4. 'Suppose you had 4 shirts and you gave one away.   How many would you have left?'
> 9. 'How many socks are in a pair of socks?'

VOCABULARY

> 1. Candle, lamp, gas jet, matches, gasoline can.
> 3. Comb, tresses, toothbrush, mouth, eye.
> 6. Bed, entrance, horse, man, window.

DIRECTIONS

> 2. 'Make a cross above the biggest circle.'   (4 circles.)
> 6. 'Put a dot below this line.'   (Pointing above line.)
> 8. 'Make a cross in the first square.'   (3 squares shown.)

APPENDIX II

SCHEME FOR RECORDING CHILD'S ATTITUDE TO TEST SITUATION

From the work with quite young children which this investigation involved, the writer was more than ever convinced of the desirability of further study of the frequency of occurrence, and the effect upon response, of various attitudes which the child may adopt toward the whole situation which is involved in a mental test. The constant aim in testing is to get a measurement of what the individual can do when his intellectual processes are working at their best on the task in question; hence the various devices employed to avoid distraction and discouragement and to motivate maximum effort. Even with older children and adults there is not much doubt that the aim just mentioned is in a few cases but imperfectly realized, either through the absence of full willingness to coöperate or through the presence of some disturbing emotional condition.

There would be fairly general agreement that difficulties of this kind become both more frequent and more marked as we proceed down to ages, say, below six years, where childish spontaneity and short attention span become more characteristic than they are at older ages. The child's lack of coöperation may vary in scope of application from a particular test item to the whole testing situation: it appears to vary in depth of feeling from a slight loss of interest to a very pronounced antipathy; it varies in explicitness of expression from such slight manifestations that it requires a keen examiner to detect them to very emphatic refusals on the part of the child accompanied, perhaps, by unmistakable signs of emotional disturbance; it may vary in persistency from a passing phase which is removable by a little tactful handling to an attitude which lasts over a number of interviews and resists every effort to remove it.

The word 'negativism' has been used as a term for non-coöperative behavior in the literature of abnormal psychology, and it might be useful to adopt it as a generic term for the various degrees and types of non-coöperation in test situations due to various combinations of the factors enumerated in the previous paragraph. If we do so, the question of clear definition becomes important owing to the tendency of the term to suggest a pathological condition and the probability that we would wish to apply it to cases and types of child behavior which could scarcely be regarded as abnormal.

On this whole matter we need much fuller information than is now available. What, for example, is the frequency of occurrence of given types of behavior of the kind we are discussing and what are the ages at which these types are most frequently found? To what extent is such behavior symptomatic of attitudes which 'carry over' into adult life? Is there any

71

clear line of distinction between 'negativistic' behavior and ordinary 'shyness'? To what extent may bodily conditions act as a causal agent? To what extent is 'negativistic' behavior due to the building up of habitual attitudes through the child's home life? Are such attitudes more frequently directed toward particular individuals or toward people in general? Are such attitudes more frequently caused in or caused by persons of one sex than by persons of the other sex? For obtaining some light on these and similar questions some form of observation and rating of the child's behavior is necessary as well as the arranging of special test situations and controls.

For the study of the somewhat narrower question of the effect of the child's attitude on his performance on mental tests, it would also appear necessary to have some sort of rating scheme for recording the child's behavior during testing. Most examiners take notes and record outstanding impressions when doing individual testing, but the usefulness of such notes would be increased if they were made according to a definite scheme. It should be possible to rate each child tested so as to provide a fairly accurate picture of the general nature of his test reaction. It is perhaps too much to hope that we will ever be able to make a mathematical 'correction' for the lowering of a child's test score through factors such as we are considering, but it should not be difficult to reach a stage where we will know a great deal more in general about the extent to which test scores are capable of being affected and feel more confidence than at present in regarding the test results of particular cases as being more or less unreliable.

Fairly full notes were taken on the test behavior of all the children tested in the investigation reported in this book, and the attempt has been made to include the various varieties of behavior observed in a coherent scheme which will be given for any suggestions it may contain for those who do further work along this line. The scheme is admittedly capable of improvement in various ways.

Before giving the scheme it may be of interest to recount briefly some of the individual cases where difficulty was encountered in obtaining or maintaining the child's coöperation and securing maximum effort. The records show that there were some thirty-five cases out of all the children tested where such difficulties were encountered. Almost all of these occurred in the three lowest age groups, and in less than half of them was the difficulty really pronounced.

Case 1. Girl, age 2.8. Difficulty in keeping her attention on the test on account of her general liveliness and ease of distraction from the test.

Case 2. Boy, age 3.2. Displayed little interest in the test, did not appear shy, refused to do any more when tests became too difficult for him.

Case 3. Boy, age 3.2. Wandered about room. So much spontaneous talking that it was not easy to get him to attend to test questions.

Case 4. Girl, age 3.3. Had to spend twenty-five minutes playing with child before she spoke a word; after this not much difficulty in applying test. Child entirely at ease on second sitting.

Case 5. Boy, age 3.7. Started well but developed attitude of antagonism and refused to continue during both first and second sittings; third sitting all right.

Case 6. Boy, age 3.8. Cried bitterly for first five minutes, after that gradually became at ease and eventually quite spontaneous and coöperative.

Case 7. Boy, age 4.10. Started with good coöperation, but when test was more than half way through appeared to lose interest and finally refused flatly to do any more.

This attitude was persisted in during two subsequent visits to the nursery, and the case was not completed. This was the most pronounced case which was encountered, and no obvious explanation was forthcoming.

Case 8. Boy, age 4.1. When his group was first visited this boy stood out as being very much frightened, and violently opposed to being taken away from the group to 'play games.' Once he was got into the testing room it was not long before his coöperation was obtained. On subsequent visits the boy became abusive because he was not again selected.

The first step in working out a scheme for recording the various varieties of test attitude, after having observed in detail just how a large number of children behave, would appear to be the selection of certain aspects of the child's behavior which are capable of being distinguished from one another and which are to be regarded as worth recording. For this purpose we have selected the following: the child's preliminary attitude, certain features of the establishment and maintenance of rapport or coöperation, the amount of spontaneity displayed by the child, and his attitude toward his own test performance. It is tempting to introduce the heading of 'attention,' but there appears to be little if any need for it if we record fully the facts about the child's coöperation. The subdivision of these headings is to some extent a matter of convenience, but of course it should be made so as to suit actual rather than logical requirements. Wherever it is possible, each subheading should be defined or illustrated by means of concrete examples of actual behavior, as even when our judgment of an attitude is based on a mere 'impression,' the impression itself is obviously based on the more or less consciously observed forms and changes of behavior which take place. In this connection the scheme we give is in need of fuller concrete illustration at a number of points.

SCHEME FOR RECORDING ATTITUDES AND BEHAVIOR IN TEST SITUATIONS

I. Preliminary attitude toward being tested.

    a. Reluctant to be tested, e.g., crying, need of much persuasion, desire for presence of a third person.

    b. Apparently indifferent to the test situation.

    c. Noticeably keen on being tested. (This preliminary attitude may mean much or little according to previous experiences, if any, of being tested.)

2. Rapidity of obtaining child's coöperation.

   a. Could not be persuaded to coöperate during sitting which lasted ...... and when ...... means were employed to put child at ease.

   b. Had to spend ...... minutes playing with or talking to child before test could be commenced.

   c. No delay in securing coöperation and starting test.

3. Type of coöperation obtained.

   a. No hesitation in doing things, but refusal or reluctance to talk.

   b. Readily distracted, e.g., by sounds outside room, test material not in use, etc.

   c. Unwilling to fall in with examiner's suggestions.

   d. Normally attentive to test and to examiner's requests.

   e. Noticeably attentive and willing, e.g., desire to do more after completion.

4. Maintenance of coöperation.

   a. Child lost interest in test situation after ...... minutes, e.g., expressed desire to discontinue.

   b. Child coöperated better as test proceeded.

   c. Steady throughout.

5. Degree of spontaneity shown by child.

   a. Child appeared to be under restraint, e.g., did not speak except when asked questions.

   b. Normally at ease.

   c. Very much at ease, e.g., sang songs, told confidences, left chair of own accord, etc.

6. Attitude toward own test performance.

   a. Mistrustful of own ability, e.g., frequent appeals for help, would not attempt some tasks.

   b. Not noticeably unusual.

   c. Very confident, e.g., use of expressions such as 'I'm sure I can do it.'